The Psychology of Stock Market Investing

Mastering Emotions and Behavioral Biases to Build Wealth

Hyun Kim CFA

Hidden Alpha Capital LLC

Disclaimer

THE INFORMATION PROVIDED IN this book is for informational purposes only and is not intended to be a source of investment and financial advice or analysis with respect to the material presented. The information and/or documents contained in this book do not constitute legal or financial advice and should never be used without first consulting with a financial professional to determine what may be best for your individual needs.

The publisher and the author do not make any guarantee or other promise as to any results that may be obtained from using the content of this book. You should never make any investment decision without first consulting with your own financial advisor and conducting your own research and due diligence. To the maximum extent permitted by law, the publisher and the author disclaim any and all liability in the event any information, commentary, analysis, opinions, advice and/or recommendations contained in this book prove to be inaccurate, incomplete or unreliable, or result in any investment or other losses.

Content contained or made available through this book is not intended to and does not constitute legal advice or investment advice and no attorney-client relationship is formed. The publisher and the author are providing this book and its contents on an "as is" basis. Your use of the information in this book is at your own risk.

Contents

Contents

Chapter One

When Brilliance Blinds Us

The $9 Billion Illusion of Elizabeth Holmes and Theranos

THE STAGE LIGHTS WERE warm. The room was packed with suits and smiles. It was September 2015, and Elizabeth Holmes, 31 years old, with piercing blue eyes and a Steve Jobs uniform, stepped up to the podium in Washington, D.C. She didn't just look confident. She looked untouchable.

Her voice was deep, deliberate. "We can run hundreds of tests on just a drop of blood," she said, holding her fingers an inch apart. The audience leaned in. No more needles. No more waiting rooms. Just a tiny nanotainer, a finger prick, and answers to your health delivered faster than Amazon Prime (Parloff, 2015).

You could feel it in the room. This wasn't a business pitch. It was a sermon. Holmes wasn't selling a product. She was promising a revolution. And nearly everyone bought in.

Not just the press. Not just Silicon Valley. Everyone. Four-star generals. Cabinet members. Billionaires. The kind of people who usually do the vetting. Her board looked like a shadow government. Her investors? Titans. Rupert Murdoch, Larry Ellison, the Walton family. Nearly $1.3 billion raised. At her peak, Forbes called her America's youngest self-made female billionaire (Herper, 2016).

But behind the stage lights and magazine covers, a very different story was unfolding.

In a quiet office across the country, a Wall Street Journal reporter named John Carreyrou was connecting the dots. Whispers. Lawsuits. Former employees too scared to speak on the record. What he found was staggering: the technology didn't work. At all. While Holmes was on stage promising miracles, her company was using third-party machines, manipulating results, and lying to doctors, regulators, and patients.

Just weeks after that dazzling speech in D.C., Carreyrou's article dropped and the façade shattered (Carreyrou, 2015).

Theranos went from a $9 billion darling to a courtroom drama. Holmes went from icon to convicted felon. By 2022, she had been sentenced to over 11 years in prison.

So what happened? Were the investors stupid? Blind? No, most were seasoned pros. They just got swept up. By a story. By the aura of genius. By the fear of missing out on the next big thing.

This isn't just a story about fraud. It's a warning shot for every investor chasing brilliance. Because sometimes, the more dazzling the dream, the harder it is to see what's missing.

And sometimes, what's missing is everything.

The Perfect Storm

Picture a room full of powerful people. Seasoned investors in bespoke suits, former secretaries of state, tech journalists with decades on the beat. All nodding along as a young woman in a black turtleneck promises to revolutionize medicine. No one asks the obvious questions. Not yet.

Elizabeth Holmes didn't need to outsmart the world to build a $9 billion mirage. She just had to tap into the glitches in our mental software, those universal psychological biases that blind even the best of us. Her genius wasn't technical; it was psychological.

What happened in that room is a classic case of the seduction of certainty. Holmes didn't hedge. "This is not a dream," she declared from the TEDMED stage in 2014. "We've done it." No qualifiers. No doubt. That kind of conviction can short-circuit skepticism. In a world filled with maybes and caveats, her certainty was disarming. Challenging her felt not just impolite. It felt almost ignorant (TEDMED, 2014).

The secrecy of Theranos only amplified the illusion. Hiding behind claims of protecting intellectual property, the company avoided the rigorous scientific scrutiny that might have exposed the truth. The silence was strategic, letting confidence do the talking.

Another layer at play was the illusion of authority, working hand in hand with the pull of social proof. Theranos' board read like a national security summit: former senators, secretaries of state, and military brass. Impressive, absolutely, but not remotely relevant. That's how you get George Shultz, a titan of diplomacy, ignoring his own grandson's whistleblower warnings to stand behind Holmes. Credentials conferred legitimacy, while real expertise went missing.

The effect was only amplified by the company's backers. Theranos wasn't just supported by wealthy investors. It was the rich: Murdoch, Walton, Ellison. Big names and even bigger bets created a feedback loop. If they were in, it had to be legit. That's the power of social proof, and it's potent. We're all susceptible. A Nobel-winning physicist muses on crypto and people listen, not because they should, but because the halo is blinding. But just because everyone is jumping off the cliff does not mean there is water below.

Holmes also understood the power of storytelling. She had the perfect origin tale. Stanford dropout, fear of needles, a mission to save lives with a pinprick. It had all the makings of a modern fairy tale, right down to the black turtlenecks meant to echo Steve Jobs. And it worked. Investors and journalists alike fell for the narrative, not the numbers. Her story made people feel good, and when a story feels true, we rarely check whether it is.

Even now, the investments I'm most confident in often have the strongest stories. That's not necessarily wrong, but when the narrative starts driving the analysis, it's time to hit pause.

Once people bought into Theranos, their brains started filtering reality to match the belief. Walgreens rolled out in-store blood tests without verifying the tech. Investors funneled millions without demanding peer-reviewed data. They saw what they wanted to see and ignored what they didn't. It's human. I've done it. Hold a stock, and suddenly every bullish article feels smart. Every bearish one feels flawed. We build echo chambers around our investments and call it conviction.

Even as the cracks appeared, investors reached the point of no return. They doubled down, adding more funding and more defenses. Admitting they were wrong wasn't just embarrassing. It was existential. Their reputations were on the line. We've all been there, backing a decision not because it's right, but because it's ours. Cutting losses feels like a failure, so we keep going, straight into the wall.

The real lesson of Theranos is not about Elizabeth Holmes. It's not even about the high-powered investors who fell for the pitch. It's about us: how even the sharpest minds can make profoundly bad decisions for reasons that have nothing to do with intelligence and everything to do with human nature.

Our brains were not built for balance sheets. They were built for survival, for fight or flight, friend or foe. The same instincts that once helped our ancestors avoid saber-toothed cats now guide our decisions on startups, stock picks, and board appointments. The tools are ancient, the context is modern, and the mismatch is dangerous.

Financial education, for all its formulas and frameworks, barely touches this reality. We're taught to value companies, not to question our own thinking. It's like giving someone a driver's manual without ever mentioning blind spots.

And here's the kicker: the smarter you are, the more vulnerable you might be. Confidence grows with success. Analysts with track records start trusting their gut. Professionals defend past calls because their reputations are on the line. What starts as expertise quietly morphs into an ego.

I've seen it everywhere, from Reddit threads to high-floor offices in Midtown Manhattan. The small-time trader clinging to a favorite ticker and the Ivy League quant rationalizing a bad bet with a spreadsheet. They are dancing to the same psychological rhythm.

Because at the core, this isn't about data. It's about identity. Once we believe something, really believe it, we don't just defend the idea. We defend ourselves.

The Real Price of Mental Blindness

The cost of falling for psychological traps in investing goes far beyond a single bad pick or a headline-grabbing blow-up like Theranos. The real damage shows up in layers. Some are obvious, others are more subtle, but all are very real.

Start with the obvious: money lost. Theranos investors alone saw nearly $700 million go up in smoke. That's capital that could have been backing real innovation, but instead it was sunk into a company selling hope dressed up as science.

And that's just one example. Look at the dot-com bust, the 2008 financial crisis, and the various crypto frenzies. The fingerprints of psychological bias are all over them. Whether it's overconfidence, herd mentality, or blind belief in a story, these mistakes scale. When they do, they don't just dent portfolios. They erase trillions in value.

Even in calmer markets, the pattern holds. Individual investors often underperform index funds not because they lack access to information, but because they make poor decisions. Buying high, selling low, overtrading, and chasing trends. It's not bad luck. It's bad psychology.

Then there's the quieter, longer-lasting loss: opportunity cost. The money you sunk into a story stock that flopped is more than just the initial hit. It's the decades of compounding you missed out on if that same capital had been in something more stable and real.

A bad decision at 35 doesn't just sting now. It echoes through your financial future. Early mistakes, especially if driven by narrative or hype, can shrink your long-term nest egg by much more than the original loss.

Psychological errors don't just cost money. They eat at you. Losing money on a calculated risk feels different from losing it on something you should have seen coming.

It's a familiar feeling. You realize you bought into a compelling story or followed the crowd, and you can't stop replaying the moment you ignored your own rules. That self-blame sticks. It makes you second-guess future decisions or swing the other way into recklessness just to make up for it. Neither path ends well.

This doesn't just happen in our portfolios. When enough people fall for the same bias, capital starts flowing to the wrong places. Whole industries get mispriced. Flashy startups with a great pitch deck but shaky fundamentals raise billions, while solid, boring companies solving real problems struggle to get attention.

With Theranos, it wasn't just the $700 million lost. It was the dozens of real healthcare startups that didn't get that funding. When the market rewards storytelling over substance, everyone pays a price.

In everyday investing roles, the same risk applies. Letting bias cloud your judgment can lead to poor performance, loss of client trust, or missed promotions. Not because you weren't smart, but because you let your brain run the show without building in any checks.

A Smarter Way to Invest: Thinking with Guardrails

It's one thing to know about behavioral biases. Most investors have heard of things like confirmation bias or overconfidence. But knowing isn't enough. If it were, none of us would fall for them, yet we do, over and over.

That's because awareness doesn't change how the brain is wired. These biases are baked into how we process the world. You can't out-think them with willpower alone.

What actually works is building systems. You need structures that catch you before you drift. You need guardrails that don't depend on how you're feeling that day. The psychologically intelligent investor isn't someone who avoids bias completely (no one can). Instead, it's someone who invests in a way that accounts for those biases and protects against them.

They use tools like pre-commitment rules, checklists before every major decision, and automated systems that take emotion out of execution. When the market is swinging wildly and everyone else is reacting on instinct, they've already decided how they'll respond, long before the storm hits.

This kind of structure becomes a real edge in volatile markets, where emotional discipline is both hardest to maintain and most valuable. While others are panicking or getting greedy, the psychologically intelligent investor sticks to a consistent, grounded process.

But getting there takes work. You need to know your own weak spots. You need to practice discipline the same way athletes practice technique, not just in theory, but in how you actually operate. Sometimes you need someone or something outside yourself (a checklist, a partner, a preset rule) to help keep you honest when your emotions try to take the wheel.

This isn't about becoming robotic. It's about building an investing approach that respects the reality of human psychology and works with it, not against it.

What This Book Will Help You Do

This book is your guide to understanding the invisible forces that quietly sabotage even the smartest investment decisions. We're going to walk through the most common psychological biases that show up in markets. Not just the dramatic blow-ups like Theranos, but also the everyday traps that sneak into your portfolio when you're not looking.

You'll see how things like loss aversion make it hard to sell a losing stock, or how recency bias leads people to believe that whatever's happening now will keep happening forever. Each chapter focuses on one of these mental missteps and unpacks it using real examples from market history, fund managers, and retail investors.

But this book isn't just about identifying the problems. It's about giving you a toolkit to fix them.

Each chapter includes practical strategies, tools, habits, and frameworks you can put to work right away. These aren't abstract theories. They are methods used by investors who've learned, often the hard way, how to put psychological guardrails in place before emotions take over.

That's why this journey isn't just about naming biases. It's about seeing how they interact and learning how to build a system that can withstand them.

By the time you reach the end, you'll have something better than a few new terms to throw around. You'll have a real-world decision-making framework built with psychology in mind, one that helps you become a more consistent, rational, and resilient investor.

Because the best investors aren't the ones who avoid mistakes. They are the ones who know how to see them coming and cut them off before they compound.

Chapter Two

Confidence That Outpaces Competence

The $1 Trillion Bet That Almost Broke the System: The Story of LTCM

T HEY WERE THE SMARTEST guys in the room. Maybe the smartest ever to walk onto Wall Street.

Long-Term Capital Management, or LTCM, wasn't your typical hedge fund. It was a financial dream team. Myron Scholes and Robert Merton had won Nobel Prizes for their work on options pricing. Their formulas had reshaped how markets thought about risk. David Mullins had been vice-chairman of the Federal Reserve. John Meriwether was a bond trading legend from Salomon Brothers.

These weren't just successful people. They were the high priests of modern finance.

When LTCM launched in 1994, investors practically begged to get in. The minimum buy-in was $10 million. Even so, they had to turn people away. In their first two years, they posted after-fee returns of 42.8 percent and 40.8 percent. Those kinds of numbers don't just attract attention. They build mythology. The performance seemed to validate what everyone already suspected: these guys had cracked the code (Lowenstein, 2000).

Their strategy was built around finding tiny price discrepancies in bond markets. Little mispricing that most investors wouldn't bother with and betting heavily that those prices would come back into line. It wasn't sexy, but it was smart. Their models, fed with mountains of historical data, said these trades were close to risk-free. One partner described it as "picking up nickels in front of a steamroller." Small, frequent, nearly certain gains. And because the trades were supposedly uncorrelated, they piled on leverage to amplify the profits.

By 1998, they weren't just managing money. They were playing with fire. LTCM had built positions with more than $1 trillion in notional value. They claimed to be market-neutral, but their leverage had ballooned to 25-to-1. For every dollar of capital, they'd borrowed twenty-five more. Everything looked good on paper. The math said the risks were minimal. But the market doesn't always follow the math.

In August of that year, Russia defaulted on its debt. It was the kind of shock that turns market assumptions upside down. Correlations between assets (the relationships that their models relied on) snapped overnight. Suddenly, all the bets they thought were independent started moving together. And they moved in the wrong direction.

In the span of just four weeks, LTCM lost $4.6 billion. Nearly all of the fund's capital was wiped out. But it wasn't just their investors who were in trouble. LTCM had grown so large, and its trades so interconnected, that its collapse threatened to destabilize the entire financial system. The Federal Reserve had to step in and coordinate a private-sector bailout to contain the fallout. In the end, the fund that once symbolized intellectual dominance was dismantled piece by piece (Dunbar, 2000).

So what went wrong?

Overconfidence. The partners at LTCM believed that they had mastered risk and that their equations could control it, even eliminate it. But in reality, they had just masked it. Their models didn't account for real-world chaos: unexpected political shocks, mass panic, and irrational market behavior. The messiness of human nature isn't something you can plug into a formula.

Warren Buffett summed it up best: "To make money they didn't have and didn't need, they risked what they did have and did need."

That's the essence of the overconfidence trap. It makes smart people take dumb risks. It convinces you that because you've been right before, you'll be right again. That you understand the game better than everyone else. And it doesn't just live in billion-dollar hedge funds. It shows up every time you hit "buy" thinking you've found the next big winner. It's there when you ignore risk because your last pick worked out.

The LTCM story isn't just a tale from the past. It is a cautionary reminder that overconfidence isn't just dangerous. It is deadly, especially in investing. The same mental bias that brought down Nobel Prize winners and Wall Street elites is lurking in all of us.

Unless you learn how to spot it, it could end up costing you more than just money.

This chapter is about that blind spot: why even brilliant investors fall for it, and how you can avoid joining the long list of people who bet too much, too confidently, and learned the hard way what they didn't know.

Why Feeling Sure Can Be So Misleading

Most investors have felt it... that rush of confidence when something just clicks. Maybe your brother-in-law in tech swore a certain startup was the next big thing. Or you read the tea leaves of some market trend and felt like you had cracked the code. Maybe it was just a gut feeling that this was the right stock, the right time, and the right play.

Often, those moments feel like turning points. But in hindsight, they are just as likely to become humbling reminders. It is surprisingly common, even for seasoned investors, to find that the ideas they feel most certain about are the ones that backfire. That kind of conviction, especially the bulletproof, nothing-can-go-wrong kind, has a nasty habit of clouding judgment. It leads us to take bigger risks, double down when we should step back, and tune out warning signs that later feel glaringly obvious.

Years ago, I got hooked on an online marketing company I thought was criminally undervalued. I pored over the numbers, loved the business model, and convinced myself the market was missing something big. I bought more than I should have and even went on margin to juice the bet.

Six months later, the stock was down 40 percent. Earnings came in weak, customers were getting harder to acquire, rivals were eating into market share, and management danced around questions from investors. The red flags were all there. I just didn't want to see them.

That's the trap. When we're sure we're right, we naturally start ignoring anything that suggests we might be wrong. Our brains filter the news. Good headlines feel like validation. Bad ones just feel like noise. Before you know it, you're neck-deep in a bad investment, wondering how you missed what now feels so obvious.

This is not just a rookie mistake. It happens to pros too. Stanford's Philip Tetlock spent decades tracking expert forecasters. His big finding was this: the more confident someone was in their predictions, the more likely they were to be wrong. The best forecasters were not the loudest or the most certain. They were the ones who kept some humility, who stayed flexible, who changed their minds when the facts changed (Tetlock, 2005).

Confidence feels good. But in the market, it can be poison. The next time you are convinced you have found a sure thing, try this: pause and ask yourself, what if I am wrong? That simple question can save you a fortune.

The Confidence Spectrum

It is important to understand that confidence is not inherently bad. In fact, it exists on a spectrum, and finding the right balance is crucial for successful investing.

The key is not to avoid confidence. It is about knowing where you sit on that spectrum and making sure you do not drift too far to either extreme.

At one end, you find crippling self-doubt. This is where investors get stuck overthinking every move. They wait for the stars to align: perfect timing, perfect valuation, and perfect conviction. But markets do not work like that. I have worked with people who spent years on the sidelines, watching great companies double or triple while their cash sat in a savings account. They were not lazy. They were just frozen by the fear of being wrong.

In the sweet spot sits healthy confidence. These investors trust their homework, make decisions with conviction, and pull the trigger when the odds are good, but they do not pretend to know the future. They stay curious. They invite dissent. They size their bets like they might be wrong, because sometimes they will be.

And then there is the other extreme: blind overconfidence. This is where things blow up. This is the Long-Term Capital Management example discussed earlier. They ignored the signals that their assumptions were breaking down. When the market turned, they did not back off. They doubled down.

The problem is, we all tend to slide in that direction. Overconfidence feels good. Certainty is comforting. Once we have a view, our brains start doing the lazy work, filtering out anything that might challenge it and spotlighting anything that confirms it. That is not a flaw. That is human wiring.

But in investing, it can be fatal.

Why We Think We Can Control the Uncontrollable

Closely tied to overconfidence is something psychologists call the illusion of control, our tendency to believe we have more influence over outcomes than we actually do. In everyday life, it is mostly harmless. In investing, it can be downright dangerous.

Markets move for reasons far beyond our reach. A central bank decision in Europe. A surprise earnings miss. A political shock on the other side of the world. These things shape our portfolios more than we care to admit. Yet we often act like we are steering the ship.

Take Stanley Druckenmiller, one of the sharpest investors of our time. During the late 1990s dot-com mania, he knew the market was frothy. He saw the bubble. But he still piled in, thinking he could ride the wave a bit longer and jump out just before the crash. "I thought we would be in the seventh or eighth inning of the tech boom. I did not know we were already in the ninth," he later said. The result was a three billion dollar loss in six weeks (Burton, 2015).

If someone with Druckenmiller's track record can fall for the illusion of control, what chance do the rest of us have?

You see this illusion everywhere. People try to time the exact top or bottom of the market. They believe they have spotted the next Tesla or Amazon. They draw patterns on charts and convince themselves they have cracked the code. Most of the time, we are not controlling the game. We are just playing in it.

That does not mean we are powerless. It just means we need to be honest about what we can control: our process, our risk, and our behavior. The rest is probabilities. Even the most well-researched idea can go sideways because of some random, out-of-nowhere event.

So no, this does not mean you have to give up and park everything in an index fund, though for most people, that is a smart move. It means we should approach the markets with humility and always be aware that we are making bets in a game where the rules can change without warning.

Why Experts Make More Mistakes

One of the sneakiest traps in investing is that the more you know, the more overconfident you can become. It seems backwards. You would think gaining experience would make you more aware of what you do not know, but often it does the opposite.

Take this story from the early 2000s. A well-known energy analyst with over thirty years in the business had built a reputation for accurately calling oil price moves. When he spoke, investors listened. Oil was trading around thirty dollars a barrel. He laid out a compelling case: rising demand from emerging markets, limited new supply, geopolitical instability, and confidently predicted oil would climb to fifty within five years.

His prediction spread quickly. Media outlets echoed it. Investors loaded up on energy stocks. It sounded smart. It sounded reasonable. And technically, he was right, but not in the way he expected.

Oil did not climb slowly to fifty. It rocketed past it. By 2008, it had hit one hundred forty-seven dollars a barrel before crashing back down in the financial crisis. The expert had not underestimated the trend. He had underestimated the volatility, the timing, and the scale. That is the point. His deep knowledge made him confident, but it also blinded him to how unpredictable markets can be.

You see this all the time. Experts make detailed calls about interest rates, GDP growth, or stock returns. They get it wrong. Not a little wrong, but sometimes wildly wrong. Yet their confidence rarely fades.

This is the Dunning-Kruger effect at the high end of the scale. It is not about beginners thinking they know more than they do. It is about seasoned experts believing their experience gives them control over outcomes that are still full of randomness. The more models and data they have, the more tempted they are to believe they have cracked the code.

Why does this happen? Because expertise builds patterns. It creates mental shortcuts that usually work until they don't. It also builds identity. Once you are known for being the oil guy or the macro forecaster, it gets harder to say, "I am not sure." Add in the comfort of past success, and you have the perfect recipe for a blind spot.

The solution is not to ignore experts. It is to think more like Howard Marks, who talks about "second-level thinking." That means going beyond the surface logic, asking how markets might react, what other investors expect, and what could go wrong even if your base case is right.

It is not about rejecting analysis. It is about remembering that even the smartest analysis is still just a guess in disguise.

Why We Take Credit for Luck and Blame Others for Losses

Another sneaky way overconfidence creeps into investing is through something psychologists call self-attribution bias. In plain English, it means we take credit when things go right, and blame someone or something else when they go wrong.

You have probably seen it play out. A stock you picked soars, and you credit your homework, your early insight, and your valuation skills. But when the same stock crashes, suddenly it is the Fed's fault. Or a black swan event. Or some hedge fund manipulating the market behind the scenes.

This kind of thinking feels harmless, even comforting. But it is dangerous. It creates a feedback loop where every win becomes proof of your genius and every loss gets brushed off as bad luck. Over time, your confidence builds on shaky ground.

I have fallen into this trap myself. During the housing-fueled bull market of the mid-2000s, I started to believe I had a knack for finding winners. The truth? A rising tide was lifting everyone's boats, and I mistook the tide for talent. It was not until the crashes, first in 2000 and then again in 2008, that I saw just how much of my "skill" had really been the market doing the heavy lifting.

So how do you stay grounded? One tool I rely on is an investing journal. Nothing fancy, just a place where I jot down why I am making a trade, what I expect to happen, and how confident I feel. Then, months or years later, I revisit it. Sometimes I am right. Often, I am wrong. But what matters is the pattern it reveals.

One of the most humbling discoveries? My most confident picks, the ones I felt bulletproof about, tended to underperform the ones I was more cautious on. After seeing that enough times, I adopted a rule: even if I feel too sure about an idea, I keep the position size below twenty percent of my portfolio. It is my way of hedging against my own blind spots.

Because in investing, the moment you are sure you cannot miss is usually the moment you are most likely to.

How Confidence Shapes Decisions Inside Companies

The confidence trap is not just a personal pitfall. It plays out in boardrooms too, often with far bigger consequences. When overconfidence infects corporate leadership, it does not just dent a portfolio. It can blow a crater in shareholder value.

Some of the worst wipeouts in business history come from executives who believed their own hype a little too much. You have seen it: bold acquisitions that made no strategic sense, sprawling expansions into unfamiliar territory, companies chasing headlines instead of profits.

A classic example is Daimler's merger with Chrysler in 1998. It was billed as a match made in automotive heaven: Germany's engineering prowess paired with America's mass-market muscle. Daimler's CEO called it a "merger of equals," but behind the scenes, confidence in the deal far outpaced the cultural and operational realities. The two companies never really meshed. Strategy clashed. Management styles collided. Within a few years, what had been sold as a transformative move unraveled into dysfunction and infighting. By 2007, Daimler unloaded Chrysler at a fraction of the original price (Stertz, 2000).

This is not a one-off. Study after study shows that most mergers (somewhere between 70% and 90%) fail to create value. Overconfident leadership is a common thread. And the bigger the deal, the more likely it is to disappoint.

But here is the good news: this is an opportunity for investors who know what to look for.

When analyzing a company, do not just read the financials. Read the room. Watch how the leadership behaves. Are they constantly making bold predictions that never quite pan out? Are they reaching far outside their core strengths with flashy acquisitions or sudden strategy pivots? For example, if a retailer suddenly wants to become a cloud computing firm, that should raise your eyebrows. The same goes for a domestic company charging into international markets without a clear plan.

Look out for "empire building." This is a classic red flag. Think sprawling new headquarters, ventures into glamorous sectors, or a string of questionable acquisitions that seem more about status than strategy. These moves often signal that the CEO is chasing size and legacy, not shareholder returns.

Warren Buffett has seen a lot in his decades at the helm of Berkshire Hathaway, including just how often mergers destroy value instead of creating it. His take: most big deals are a win for almost everyone involved, except the acquiring shareholders.

He is especially wary of CEOs who let ego and animal spirits drive the decision. As he put it, "Many CEOs attain their positions in part because they possess an abundance of animal spirits and ego... When such a CEO is encouraged by his advisors to make deals, he responds much as would a teenage boy who is encouraged by his father to have a normal sex life. It's not a push he needs." That is Buffett in classic form: blunt, humorous, and dead-on (Buffett, 1990).

On the other hand, most successful companies are run by leaders who are refreshingly grounded. They do not pretend to have all the answers. They talk openly about risks, admit when things go wrong, and do not overreach.

Jeff Bezos used to dedicate sections of Amazon's shareholder letters to what the company got wrong. Buffett and Munger have practically turned mistake-admitting into an art form. That kind of humility is not weakness. It is wisdom. It signals a culture of clear thinking, rational decision-making, and long-term focus.

In the market, that is a real competitive edge.

How Different Cultures Think About Confidence

It is also worth recognizing that overconfidence does not look the same everywhere. Depending on where you invest or who you invest with, it can show up in very different ways. These cultural flavors of confidence shape not just the risks we take, but the kinds of opportunities we chase.

Take Silicon Valley, for example. In the world of venture capital, confidence is not just accepted. It is a prerequisite. The whole game is built around moonshots. Most bets are expected to fail. The hope is that one outlier, one Uber or one Airbnb, pays for the rest. Founders pitch bold visions with near-religious certainty. VCs nod along, knowing that a little delusion might be part of the formula.

In that environment, being cautiously optimistic will not get you funded. The system rewards big, bold bets, and every now and then, that extreme optimism turns out to be right. But it also creates a landmine of inflated valuations and startup flameouts. If you are investing in that world, you have to accept that the signal is wrapped in a lot of noise.

Now compare that to the world of value investing, with its roots in Omaha and Warren Buffett's approach. Here, confidence wears a different mask. It is quieter, more analytical. Investors pride themselves on staying within their "circle of competence," buying only when the odds feel overwhelmingly in their favor. The ideal investment is the "fat pitch," an obvious winner, bought at a clear discount.

But even here, overconfidence can sneak in. It might not sound like bravado, but it shows up as belief in your own superior analysis. Value investors can convince themselves they have uncovered hidden value the market somehow missed, even when they are just seeing what everyone else sees through a slightly rosier lens.

Neither culture is right or wrong. They just operate by different rules. The key is to understand the water you are swimming in. If you spend your time in growth-focused circles, you might need to check your optimism. If you are deep in value investing, maybe check whether your edge is real or just imagined.

Because at the end of the day, the risk is not just being overconfident. It is being overconfident without realizing it and letting the culture around you amplify that blind spot.

The Final Word: Confident Enough to Act, Humble Enough to Learn

If there is one trap that quietly haunts every investor, it is overconfidence. Not the loud, chest-thumping kind you see in bull markets, but the subtler kind: the craving for certainty in a world that rarely offers it.

Markets are not clean puzzles waiting to be solved. They are messy, noisy, and full of surprises. Trying to predict every twist and turn with precision is not just unrealistic. It sets you up for disappointment.

But here is the thing: you do need confidence to invest. You need it to make decisions, to take smart risks, and to build conviction. The trick is aiming for the right kind of confidence, the kind that does not crumble when you are wrong. It is not about being sure. It is about being steady.

That kind of confidence starts with humility. Real humility. The kind that says, "I have done the work, but I still might be missing something." It is the humility that understands your analysis is only as good as your assumptions, and that markets have a way of making fools of us all at some point.

Warren Buffett gets this balance better than anyone. Despite decades of outperformance, he is quick to admit what he does not know. One of his favorite sayings, borrowed from physicist Richard Feynman, is, "There is a difference between knowing the name of something and knowing something." That mindset and intellectual humility do not make him timid. It makes him sharp. He sticks to his "circle of competence," and that is exactly why he has earned the right to act boldly when the odds are in his favor.

The irony is that when you invest with this kind of balanced mindset, you often make better decisions. You do not panic when the market drops. You do not cling to bad trades out of ego. You stay curious. You adapt. You keep going.

Slowly, your edge compounds, not just in returns, but in judgment.

Because here is what the market will teach you, again and again: the moment you are sure of something is usually the moment you should take a step back. Certainty can be dangerous. Doubt, used wisely, can be your ally.

So move forward with conviction, but hold your beliefs with a light grip. Be ready to adjust. Do not be afraid to say, "I do not know."

That is not a weakness. In this game, it might just be your greatest strength.

Chapter Three

Luck, Mistaken for Skill

B ACK IN 2007, BILL Miller could do no wrong. He was the guy every investor wanted to be. As the manager of the Legg Mason Value Trust, he had beaten the S&P 500 for 15 straight years. That's not just rare. It was practically unheard of. He was on magazine covers. Investment conferences treated him like a rock star. People wanted to reverse-engineer his strategy, hoping they could bottle that success.

Then 2008 hit.

The financial crisis tore through the markets, and Miller's fund got hammered down 55%, trailing the market by 18 percentage points. The same media that once praised his brilliance now questioned whether he'd lost his touch. Money flooded out of his fund. The winning streak wasn't just over. It had been obliterated (Goldstein, 2008).

But here's the part that's easy to miss: Miller didn't suddenly start making reckless bets. His strategy hadn't really changed. What had changed was the environment. For years, his concentrated positions in financial stocks had worked beautifully. But when that sector imploded, so did his portfolio. It wasn't that he became foolish overnight. It's that the tide went out.

What made it worse was the illusion that his success was universal and that a 15-year streak meant the strategy would hold up in any environment. That illusion wasn't just in the headlines or among investors. It can creep in quietly, even for the person managing the portfolio. A strategy that worked under certain conditions was mistaken for all-weather brilliance. And when the cycle turned, those hidden risks were exposed.

This story is a stark reminder of one of the most persistent investing biases out there: the illusion of skill. We love to credit ourselves when things go well. "I knew that stock would take off!" But when the wheels fall off? Suddenly it's the Fed's fault, or the market's irrationality, or some unforeseen event no one could have predicted.

And this bias doesn't just show up in how we view the pros. It hits closer to home. It affects how we judge our own decisions. We chalk up every win to our insight and every loss to bad luck. That kind of thinking is dangerous. It encourages us to double down on strategies that may have worked for reasons we don't fully understand. It builds overconfidence and sets the stage for much bigger setbacks down the road.

The truth is, in investing, skill and luck are often tangled together. And the difference between the two sometimes only becomes clear after the fact. Staying humble and being brutally honest with yourself about why something worked is one of the best ways to protect your portfolio from your own ego.

How to Tell If Success Comes from Skill or Luck

One of the trickiest things in investing is separating skill from luck. And to really understand how the illusion of skill leads us astray, we have to recognize that different types of investment activities fall at different points along what I think of as a skill-luck spectrum.

At one end of the spectrum, you have activities that are almost entirely driven by chance. These include things like short-term price movements, trying to call market tops and bottoms, guessing where currencies are headed, or attempting to nail earnings down to the penny. Day trading, too, often lives in this camp. These are areas where even the most thoughtful decision-making can be overwhelmed by randomness. You might be right, but more often than not, it's luck (good or bad) that determines the outcome.

Then there's the middle of the spectrum and zones where both luck and skill play meaningful roles. This is where things like stock picking over a few months, moving between asset classes, or rotating between sectors come into play. Picking a fund manager can also fall here. You can have skillful inputs (sound reasoning, solid analysis) but the results still depend heavily on timing and external factors.

Finally, at the far end, we have the parts of investing that are most influenced by real skill. Things like building a long-term strategic asset allocation, sticking to a thoughtful investment process, managing your costs, keeping your emotions in check, harvesting tax efficiencies, and managing risk responsibly. These are not sexy, and they won't make headlines, but over time, they are the cornerstones of good investing. They don't rely on guessing what will happen next. They are about being prepared no matter what happens.

The problem is, in areas where luck dominates, the feedback we get from outcomes is misleading. You can make a bad call, say, buying a stock on a hot tip without any research, and still get a great return if that stock happens to spike because of a takeover or some short-term hype. That's dumb luck, but it feels like skill. On the flip side, you might do everything right, analyze a business thoroughly, buy at a fair price, and still lose money because something unexpected derails the company. That's bad luck, but it feels like a failure.

The real challenge is that outcomes are loud and obvious. They hit our brokerage accounts and emotions in real time. But process? That's quiet. It requires reflection and honesty. It doesn't show up on the chart. And because of that imbalance, because results are so visible and seductive, we tend to focus on them and forget to ask whether our thinking made sense in the first place.

Over time, the best investors are not the ones who get lucky the most. They are the ones who learn to judge the quality of their process, not just the outcome.

The Two Faces of the Illusion

One of the most deceptive traps in investing is thinking we're smarter than we are. And often, this illusion of skill isn't just about one bad habit. It's powered by two biases working hand in hand.

The first is outcome bias. It's our tendency to judge the quality of a decision based entirely on how things turned out. If we make money, we assume we made a smart call. If we lose money, we blame a poor decision. But investing doesn't work like that. In the short run, bad decisions can make you money, and good ones can lose you plenty. Markets are noisy. Outcomes aren't always a fair scorecard.

I saw this play out with a friend who jumped into crypto at the end of 2020. He didn't know much about blockchain or tokenomics. He just sensed it was the next big thing. When prices took off in 2021, he patted himself on the back for his bold, forward-looking "strategy." But when the crash came in 2022, it was clear he'd simply gotten lucky during a massive bull run. His process hadn't changed. The only thing that had changed was the result.

Then there's hindsight bias, which often shows up right behind it. This is the sneaky feeling that, after something happens, we "knew it all along." How many times have you heard (or said), "I knew that stock was going to tank," or "I had a feeling the market was due for a correction"?

Together, these two biases (outcome bias and hindsight bias) create a dangerous feedback loop. We take too much credit when things go right. Then we convince ourselves we saw it coming. And before long, we start believing we've got a special edge. That's when over-confidence creeps in. We take bigger risks, bet heavier, assume our instincts are sharper than they are. Until, eventually, reality shows up and reminds us that luck runs both ways.

The trick isn't to eliminate these biases. They're baked into how our brains work. But if we can spot them when they show up, we stand a much better chance of staying humble, staying rational, and staying in the game.

Bias in Action: The Day Trader's Delusion

Few areas in investing reveal the illusion of skill more clearly than day trading. It's easy to see why the idea is so appealing: the freedom to work from anywhere, quick wins, and the promise of controlling your financial future with just a laptop and a few clicks. The dream is seductive, but the data tells a much tougher story.

Brad Barber and Terrance Odean, professors at the University of California, have spent years studying individual investors and day traders. Their research is some of the most extensive in the field, and the results are sobering. In one of their most cited studies, they tracked the performance of thousands of day traders over a 15-year period in Taiwan, a country with one of the most active day trading communities in the world. What they found was striking: day traders, on average, lost money every single year. Not just occasionally... every year. Nearly 80% of traders lost money, and only a tiny fraction showed any sustained profitability.

And even among those few who had winning stretches, success rarely lasted. Barber and Odean found that the traders who did well in one period almost never repeated that performance later. In other words, what looked like skill was mostly luck. With enough people flipping coins, someone's bound to hit a streak of heads, but that doesn't make them an expert at coin tossing.

Their research also showed a clear pattern: the more frequently investors traded, the worse they performed. In a study of U.S. investors, Barber and Odean discovered that the most active traders, those most confident in their skill, underperformed the market by around 6.5% a year after accounting for transaction costs. The more someone believed in their edge, the more damage they tended to do (Odean, 2000).

This illusion of skill is especially persistent in day trading because of how the game is structured. You get constant feedback. A few early wins, and you start believing you've figured it out. Losses? Those must be flukes... bad luck, market manipulation, or just a bump in the road. That kind of thinking creates a dangerous feedback loop:

random success breeds confidence, which leads to increased risk-taking, and eventually, painful losses.

Despite all this, millions continue to believe they can out-trade the market. The occasional winning streak keeps the hope alive, like a slot machine that pays out just enough to keep you pulling the lever. But what Barber and Odean's research shows again and again is that most of those wins are statistical noise. They're not the result of some special insight or edge. They're what happens when chance occasionally hands someone a lucky break.

The lesson isn't that no one should ever trade. It's that we need to be brutally honest with ourselves about whether our results reflect true skill or if we're just riding a wave of randomness, we happened to catch. Because the market doesn't care how confident we feel. And it doesn't hand out second chances when the luck runs dry.

The CEO Celebrity Trap: When Leadership Hype Outshines Business Reality

When you're picking stocks, it's easy to get drawn into stories about visionary CEOs. The business press loves to build these narratives. This one person saved a company. That one turned a dinosaur into a disruptor. But often, those stories oversimplify what's really going on. They ignore timing, industry trends, and good old-fashioned luck.

Take Hubert Joly, for example. When he took the reins at Best Buy in 2012, the company looked like it was heading for the same fate as other brick-and-mortar retailers buried by Amazon. But then something surprising happened. Best Buy didn't just survive. It rallied. The stock surged. Joly was praised as a retail mastermind, the man who "saved" the company.

Now, Joly absolutely made smart moves. He improved operations, revitalized stores, and focused on customer service. But his success didn't happen in a vacuum. Around the same time, Best Buy's biggest competitors, Circuit City and RadioShack, were going under. That cleared the playing field. And consumers, helped by a strong economy, started spending again. It was a turnaround, yes but it was helped along by some pretty favorable conditions (Wahba, 2019).

This kind of story plays out again and again. We love to give all the credit to the person at the top, but we often ignore the backdrop. The risk, as investors, is that we buy into the myth of the irreplaceable CEO, without asking whether the business itself is built to last.

So before jumping into a company because its leader is being celebrated in the headlines, take a closer look. Is the business strong across different market cycles, or has it only done well during good times? Does it have real, structural advantages, or has it just been in the right place at the right time?

This became especially relevant during the pandemic. Companies like Zoom, Peloton, and Teladoc saw explosive growth in 2020 and 2021. Their CEOs were suddenly front-page material, celebrated for their "vision." But in truth, much of that success was circumstantial, driven by lockdowns, remote work, and a temporary shift in consumer behavior. When the world began to normalize, those tailwinds faded. And the stock prices of those same companies came back down to earth, hard.

What's lasted through all of this? The businesses with true staying power, those built on durable advantages, not just leadership charisma or temporary surges in demand. Those are the companies that tend to reward patient investors over time. The rest? They often turn out to be stories with a great first chapter... and a disappointing ending.

The Expert Problem: When Experience Doesn't Guarantee Skill

One of the more uncomfortable lessons I've had to learn over time is something I call the expert problem. In most fields, experience reliably leads to expertise. A surgeon who's done thousands of procedures is better than one who's just starting out. A pilot with decades in the cockpit is more skilled than someone fresh out of training. In those worlds, practice really does make perfect.

But investing is different.

The financial markets live in a domain where luck plays a massive role. That makes it harder to translate experience into consistent out-performance. Study after study shows that even professional money managers (people with teams of analysts, high-powered software, and years of experience) rarely beat the market over long periods. It's not that they're bad at their jobs. It's just that markets are remarkably efficient. Information moves fast. Edges vanish quickly. No amount of time in the market can change that fundamental reality.

Despite this, the financial industry often sells the idea that more years mean more skill. And it's easy to believe. I've felt it in myself. After fifteen years of investing, there are moments when I catch myself thinking, "I've seen this before. I know how this will play out." But the data and more than a few humbling trades suggest otherwise. Especially for predicting short-term market moves, experience doesn't seem to give you any special powers.

That's not to say experience is worthless. It still plays a huge role in building emotional discipline. It teaches you to manage risk more thoughtfully and stick to a process when things get rough. It helps you stay calm when the market gets noisy. But it's crucial to know where its value ends.

In investing, more time in the game doesn't always mean you've figured out the rules. Sometimes, all it means is that you've seen a lot of randomness up close, and the best thing you can do is stay humble in the face of it.

The Final Word: Focus on What You Can Control

If there's one idea to carry forward from all this, it's that the most enduring edge in investing isn't access to better data or faster tech. It's understanding human nature: yours and everyone else's. Markets evolve, algorithms get sharper, information moves at the speed of light. But human behavior? That doesn't change.

That's where the real opportunity lies. The investor who can stay calm when others panic, think clearly when stories get loud, and stick to a good process when emotions are boiling holds an edge that doesn't fade with time. It's not flashy, but it's real. And it compounds.

Michael Mauboussin captures this perfectly in The Success Equation: "When we have a lot of skill, we have a lot of control, and when we have a lot of luck, we have little control." In a field like investing, where luck and skill are always dancing together, the smartest move is to double down on what you can control.

You can't control where the market's headed next. You can't predict the next earnings miss, the next rate hike, or the next geopolitical shock. But here's what you can do: stick to a consistent process. Keep your costs low. Stay diversified. Control your emotions. Keep learning. These are the dials you actually get to turn.

When I look back on my own investing journey, my best moments didn't come from catching the perfect wave or picking the one stock that doubled. They came from staying disciplined when it was hardest. Not chasing headlines. Not panicking. Just sticking to a plan, day in and day out. That wasn't luck. That was behavior. And behavior, thankfully, is something we can shape.

This mindset shift from trying to predict outcomes to managing your process is how you sidestep the illusion of control. You stop chasing certainty and start preparing for uncertainty. You acknowledge that luck plays a part, but you don't let it trick you into thinking it's all luck or all skill.

Take Bill Miller, who we talked about at the beginning. For 15 years, he beat the market. Then came 2008, and everything fell apart. Was he a genius? A fraud? Neither. His track record had both luck and skill in the mix, just like every investor's. And after the dust settled, he came back. Not because he avoided losses, but because he kept playing the long game.

As you walk your own path, remember this: stay humble. Own what you don't know. Let short-term results be just that. Short-term. And put all your energy into the parts you can shape. Your habits. Your decisions. Your ability to stay steady when others are spinning.

You'll never eliminate luck. But if you build a system you trust and stick to it, you can outlast it. And over time, that's what separates the investors who endure from the ones who burn out.

In the end, it's not about genius. It's about resilience. And that's an edge no market can take away.

Chapter Four

Seeing Only What You Want to Believe

IN 2015, VALEANT PHARMACEUTICALS looked like a rocket ship. Under CEO Michael Pearson, it had transformed from a relatively obscure drugmaker into a Wall Street darling. Its stock had exploded more than 1,000% in just six years, driven by a bold strategy: buy up other drug companies, gut their R&D, and hike prices on existing medications, often by hundreds of percent. It wasn't innovation; it was financial engineering. And for a while, it worked (McLean, 2016).

Investors were hooked. Big-name hedge funds loaded up, none more visibly than Bill Ackman's Pershing Square. Ackman didn't just invest. He preached. He called Valeant "a very early-stage Berkshire Hathaway" and bet that it would become the most valuable pharmaceutical company in the world. His stake eventually made up about 10% of his fund (Gara, 2015).

But then the cracks started to show.

Short sellers and journalists began asking uncomfortable questions. Valeant's close relationship with a specialty pharmacy called Philidor raised red flags. Some claimed the company was using it to inflate sales. Others pointed to price hikes on life-saving drugs that sparked public outrage. Then came whispers of accounting tricks.

Instead of reassessing, Ackman doubled down. Literally. As the stock slid, he bought more. When critics raised legitimate concerns, he dismissed them, convinced they simply didn't "get it." He clung to the bullish narrative, tuning out anything that didn't support it (Boyd, 2015) (Stevenson, 2015).

That's when confirmation bias took the wheel. Ackman, like many smart investors before him, fell into the trap of believing his original thesis so strongly that he ignored the growing pile of evidence against it.

The fallout was brutal. Valeant's stock collapsed by 97%, wiping out more than $80 billion in market value. Ackman, who had been buying around $196 a share, finally exited at about $11. The total loss for his fund? Roughly $4 billion (Vardi, 2017).

This wasn't just a bad trade. It was a cautionary tale. A sharp investor got caught in his own echo chamber, filtering reality through the lens of conviction. In doing so, he mistook stubbornness for strength. Confirmation bias doesn't just cloud your thinking. In the markets, it can cost you everything.

The Invisible Filter

The Valeant fiasco wasn't just about a flawed company. It was about a deeply human flaw that even the smartest investors struggle to avoid: confirmation bias. It's one of the most stubborn mental traps in investing, because it works silently behind the scenes, shaping what we see and, more dangerously, what we don't.

At its core, confirmation bias is the tendency to embrace information that supports what we already believe and ignore anything that doesn't. Once you decide a company is a winner, your brain goes to work filtering reality to fit that view. Positive headlines? Easy to accept. Bad news? That must be a misunderstanding. This happens automatically. You're not trying to be blind. You just don't realize the blinders are on.

Think about what usually happens after you buy a stock. You start rooting for it. You seek out news and analysis that confirm your decision, and you instinctively push aside anything negative. Maybe you say the critic "doesn't understand the business." Maybe you call the bad quarter a "blip" or tell yourself it's just the market being irrational. You find reasons to believe you're still right.

This kind of mental filtering can be costly. A warning sign gets brushed off as "noise." A legitimate threat is reframed as a buying opportunity. Piece by piece, you build a case that holds together in your mind, but not in the real world. That's exactly what happened with

Valeant. The red flags were there. But many investors, locked into their thesis, and explained them away. The more the stock dropped, the more convinced they became that everyone else was wrong.

And here's the kicker: experience doesn't always help. In fact, seasoned investors might be more vulnerable. When you've been right a lot in the past, you start to trust your instincts more than the data. You think you can tell signal from noise better than others. That confidence makes it even easier to dismiss information that challenges your view.

Fighting confirmation bias takes effort. It means building habits that force you to consider the other side. Reading bear cases on your favorite holdings. Following smart investors you often disagree with. Asking yourself, "What would make me sell?" and actually answering. It's uncomfortable, but that discomfort is the point. It's a sign you're doing the work most investors avoid.

You can't erase confirmation bias completely. It's baked into how our brains work. But you can recognize it and build systems to keep it from wrecking your portfolio. The best investors aren't the ones who are always right. They're the ones who can admit when they're wrong, before the market forces them to. Often, the most valuable insight is the one you least want to hear.

The Three Mechanisms of Confirmation Bias

Confirmation bias isn't just a mental hiccup. It's a full-on system our brains run without asking for permission. In investing, it can quietly sabotage your judgment before you even realize it's happening. It works through three powerful psychological mechanisms: selective exposure, biased interpretation, and selective recall. Together, they form a feedback loop that reinforces what we already believe, regardless of whether it's still true.

It starts with selective exposure. We naturally gravitate toward information that supports our current views and steer clear of anything that might challenge them. If you're bullish on a stock, you'll probably read the bullish analysts, follow like-minded investors, and ignore the critics. That's not just comfort-seeking. It's how echo chambers form. In the digital age, with algorithms feeding us more of what we click on, that echo gets louder fast.

Then comes biased interpretation. Even when we look at the same data, we don't all see the same thing. Say a company reports lower revenue but higher earnings. A bullish investor might see improving margins and efficiency. A bearish one sees slipping demand and weakness ahead. Both are looking at the same numbers, but their minds interpret the story differently based on what they already believe. This extends even to vague statements. When a CEO says they're "exploring strategic alternatives," one side hears "exciting acquisition," the other hears "desperate exit plan."

Finally, selective recall ensures that, over time, we remember the evidence that supported our thesis and quietly forget what didn't. Our memories aren't neutral. They favor information that fits our narrative. Studies have shown that when people are presented with mixed evidence, they later recall mostly what aligned with their original views and genuinely believe they saw a one-sided case. That's not dishonesty. It's just how the human brain works.

And that's the real danger. This cycle of selective exposure, biased interpretation, and selective recall becomes stronger, the more conviction we have. The deeper we're in, the harder it is to hear anything that suggests we might be wrong. That's exactly what happened to Bill Ackman with Valeant. The facts changed. The story cracked. But confirmation bias kept him doubling down, filtering out bad news and rationalizing red flags until the stock collapsed.

In investing, conviction is a strength, but only if it's tethered to reality. The moment it turns into a filter that screens out inconvenient truths, it becomes a liability. Recognizing these mental traps isn't about weakness. It's about staying sharp. The best investors don't avoid confirmation bias. They fight it, every day, with humility and discipline.

The Buffett-Munger Partnership Model and Bridgewater's Radical Transparency

If confirmation bias is hard-wired into our thinking, how do some of the best investors in the world fight it? Two of the most successful investment organizations, Berkshire Hathaway and Bridgewater Associates, offer two very different, but equally powerful, answers.

At Berkshire, Warren Buffett and Charlie Munger have spent over six decades sharpening each other's thinking. Their edge doesn't come from flashy tools or complicated models. It comes from consistent, rigorous, and respectful disagreement. As Munger puts it: "We both try to be consistently rational. And we've learned that it works better if you have somebody to talk to instead of just talking to yourself."

They challenge each other, not to win arguments, but to find the truth. Munger loves to say that if you can't argue the other side of your idea better than your opponent, you shouldn't be proud of your opinion. That mindset keeps ego in check and turns disagreement into a feature, not a flaw. Buffett has often credited Munger for shifting his thinking, especially on the value of owning great businesses at fair prices instead of just cheap ones with shaky futures.

While Buffett and Munger approach truth-seeking with quiet discipline, Ray Dalio's Bridgewater takes it to the extreme. His firm runs on "radical transparency" and "thoughtful disagreement," and it's baked into every part of the culture. Meetings are recorded. Feedback is immediate and brutally honest. Even the founder isn't above critique. A junior employee once emailed Dalio to say his presentation was "rambling and disorganized." Dalio didn't hide the note. He shared it company-wide as proof the system was working.

At Bridgewater, hierarchy doesn't protect your ideas. Merit does. Everyone, from interns to top brass, is expected to challenge assumptions, including their own. Dalio's core belief is that ego and blind spots are the biggest barriers to good decision-making. His solution? Build a culture that forces those barriers into the light (Dalio, 2017).

You might not run a hedge fund or sit across from a Charlie Munger, but the principles behind these systems are surprisingly universal. Whether it's a trusted friend who isn't afraid to poke holes in your thesis, or a personal habit of actively seeking out opposing views, the goal is the same: stop living in an echo chamber. Confirmation bias thrives in silence. It shrinks when ideas are tested, prodded, and made to earn their place.

So ask yourself: who's challenging your thinking? What are you doing to break the feedback loop that tells you that you're always right?

In Dalio's words, "The biggest tragedy of mankind comes from the inability of people to have thoughtful disagreement to find out what's true." In investing, as in life, the ability to think clearly often depends on your willingness to be challenged.

The Double-Edged Sword

While confirmation bias can cloud our judgment, that doesn't mean conviction is the enemy. In fact, conviction, the ability to stick with a well-reasoned investment through rough patches, is often what separates great investors from those who sell at the first sign of red ink.

The danger isn't in conviction itself. It's in blind conviction, the kind that filters out inconvenient facts, dismisses all critics, and confuses stubbornness with strength. It feels good in the moment because it protects your ego. But it can quietly detach you from reality, leading you to hold on to losers far too long.

What you want instead is informed conviction. That's the kind of conviction that's earned. It means doing your homework, stress-testing your thesis, and this part's key—actively seeking out arguments that could prove you wrong. If you can hear the other side, fully understand it, and still come away with confidence, that's real conviction. It's not fragile. It's not based on hope. It's grounded.

That's the mindset that defines many of the greats. Look at Seth Klarman at Baupost. He's famous for holding positions for years, often while the market mocks him, only to be proven right long after the headlines moved on. But here's what people miss: when the facts change, he changes his mind. Quickly. No drama, no denial. What looks like stubbornness from the outside is actually disciplined thinking, a clear line between sticking to your guns and knowing when to holster them (Klarman, 1991).

So the question isn't "Do I have conviction?" It's "Is my conviction earned or assumed?" If it's earned, you'll be able to hold through the noise and make smart decisions under pressure. If it's not, it's just confirmation bias in disguise. And the market has a cruel way of exposing that.

Watch Out When Stock Picking: Confirmation Bias Isn't Just Yours

When digging into individual stocks, it's not just your own confirmation bias you need to worry about. The company's has an impact too. A big part of investment due diligence is reading between the lines: how management handles pressure, criticism, and changing realities can tell you more than any press release.

Start with how executives respond to tough questions. On earnings calls, do they engage with analysts in a thoughtful, data-driven way, or do they get defensive, pivoting away from uncomfortable topics and repeating the same talking points? That kind of evasiveness can be a red flag. It often signals a leadership team more interested in protecting their narrative than confronting inconvenient facts.

You'll also want to keep an eye on "metric-shifting." This is when a company changes which performance metric it highlights, conveniently focusing on whatever looks best that quarter. One quarter it's revenue growth, the next it's profit margins, then it's user engagement. This sleight of hand suggests they're managing perception, not performance. Netflix did something like this in 2022. After years of touting subscriber growth, it suddenly pivoted to "revenue per member" just as subscriber numbers started falling for the first time in a decade (Kafka, 2022).

Another red flag: leaders who never admit mistakes and always blame external forces (macro headwinds, regulators, competitors) for poor results. If management cannot acknowledge errors or adjust when the facts change, you're looking at institutional confirmation bias. That can drag a company down from the top.

Look at General Electric under Jeff Immelt. For years, the company painted a rosy picture while quietly stumbling. Immelt surrounded himself with like-minded executives and rarely heard dissent. That closed-off culture masked deep structural problems until it was too late. GE's stock cratered, and one of the world's most iconic industrial giants was forced to break itself apart (Mann, 2020).

Finally, consider who's sitting around the decision-making table. Diverse leadership teams with varied backgrounds, experiences, and viewpoints are more likely to challenge assumptions and avoid group thinking. Homogeneous teams may look unified, but that unity can come at the cost of perspective.

As investors, we often focus on numbers. But the narrative (how companies tell their story, respond to pressure, and handle criticism) is just as revealing. If everyone at the top is always right, always aligned, and always shifting the spotlight to whatever looks good, it's worth asking: what are they not seeing, or not willing to admit?

The Balanced Investor: Conviction Without Blindness

Beating confirmation bias doesn't mean tossing out conviction or second-guessing yourself into paralysis. The real goal is something much harder and much more powerful. It's what psychologist Philip Tetlock calls active open-mindedness: holding strong views, but staying genuinely open to evidence that might prove you wrong (Tetlock, 2015).

The best investors walk this tightrope every day. They act with confidence based on what they know, but they leave room for what they don't know. They're constantly updating their thinking as new information rolls in. F. Scott Fitzgerald described this mindset best: "The ability to hold two opposed ideas in the mind at the same time, and still retain the ability to function." (Fitzgerald, 1936)

This balance is what keeps you sharp. It helps you avoid the two extremes that sink portfolios: being so uncertain you never act, or so convinced you stop listening. It lets you make decisions with clarity while still evolving your view as the facts change.

That only happens when you've built habits that challenge your own thinking regularly, systematically, and without ego.

This is the difference between being committed and being locked in. Bill Ackman's fall with Valeant wasn't a failure of intelligence. It was a failure of flexibility. He stopped questioning his own thesis, and by the time the truth was undeniable, it was too late.

The important thing you need to remember is the market doesn't care about you and how smart you are. It only rewards those who can adapt, who can hear what they need to hear, not just what they want to hear.

That's the real edge: conviction with humility, action with self-awareness, belief tempered by doubt. It's not easy, but it's how you build real, lasting success.

Chapter Five

When Stories Trump Reality

Back in January 2000, something big happened. AOL and Time Warner announced a $165 billion merger, the largest of its kind at the time. Wall Street loved it. The media ate it up. Investors rushed in as if it were the next gold rush. On the surface, it looked like a perfect match: AOL, the internet's golden child, teaming up with Time Warner, the heavyweight in content. Together, they were supposed to dominate the digital future.

The pitch was irresistible. AOL had the distribution, those internet pipes we all used to dial into. Time Warner had the content: magazines, movies, and television. The idea was that, soon, you would be reading Time magazine or watching HBO shows straight through your AOL account. A new media empire for a new millennium. The CEOs, Steve Case and Gerald Levin, played the part of visionaries. And for a while, people believed them.

But just three years later, the dream turned into a write-down, $99 billion evaporated, the biggest corporate write-off in history at the time. The stock cratered. Over 80 percent gone. The visionaries? Out of the picture. By 2009, the companies split up, with AOL spun off like a forgotten afterthought, worth less than a rounding error compared to the original deal (Swisher, 2003).

So what happened? Simple: the story was great, but reality was stubborn. These two companies had completely different cultures and business models. They never meshed. The promised "synergies" never showed up. And while everyone was busy celebrating the narrative, the world changed. High-speed broadband rolled out quicker than anyone expected, and AOL's dial-up service became yesterday's news.

This is not just a tale of a bad merger. It is a cautionary story about how seductive a good narrative can be. When the story is strong enough, people stop asking tough questions. We overlook the hard truths. Even seasoned executives and investors fall into this trap.

Psychologists call it the narrative fallacy. We love a tidy story. We crave meaning. But in investing, the real world does not always fit into a neat little arc. And when we let the story drive the decision, rather than the facts, we open the door to some very expensive mistakes.

We have all been there. It is not just a Wall Street problem. It is human nature.

The Power of Narratives: Why Our Brains Crave Stories

To really grasp why we fall so hard for stories, especially in investing, you have to understand how our brains work. We are not wired to think in spreadsheets. We are wired to think in stories.

From the days when our ancestors sat around fires sharing hunting tales, stories helped us make sense of the world. They gave us meaning, memory, and a way to understand cause and effect. That has not changed. Whether it is a Netflix show or a pitch deck, we still absorb the world through narrative.

Stories give us a sense of "why." Why did something happen? What does it mean? That feels natural to us. It is how we make sense of uncertainty. A well-told story also hits us emotionally. It sticks. It moves us. You hear a compelling vision and suddenly you are not just thinking. You are feeling. That emotional pull can be powerful. Dangerous, too.

On top of that, stories are just easier to process. They are simpler than reality, which is usually messy, complicated, and full of trade-offs. A good story cleans that up. It gives us a clear arc: beginning, middle, and end. Our brains reward that with less cognitive strain. We can relax into the narrative, while data forces us to work.

And because stories are so easy to remember, they win the battle for mind share when we are making decisions. Facts fade. Stories stick.

This is where it gets risky in investing. Because the real world, especially in business, is rarely as neat as the stories suggest. Narratives reduce the complexity of markets, management, and technology into something bite-sized and often misleading.

Take this example. Imagine you hear two versions of the same investment idea.

The story pitch goes: "This company is using AI to revolutionize healthcare. The founder's a genius. Their tech is going to transform how we diagnose disease. Cheaper, faster, better. It's a trillion-dollar industry. Total game-changer."

Now here's the dry, data-heavy version: "They've built an AI model that analyzes medical images with 87 percent accuracy in trials. Revenue is growing 42 percent year over year, but it is still just $28 million. They lost $45 million last year and are burning cash. Several other startups and legacy players are building similar tools."

Which one are you more likely to remember? Which one pulls you in?

That is the problem. Our minds reach for the story, not the spreadsheet. But when you are investing, the spreadsheet matters more. The story can inspire, but the numbers tell you what you are actually buying. If you forget that, the story might just end with your money disappearing.

The Two Dimensions of Narrative Bias

Narrative bias tends to sneak into our thinking in two major ways: by oversimplifying complexity and by causing us to ignore inconvenient facts. These two forces feed off each other, often without us even realizing it.

First, there is narrative simplification. Investing involves navigating a messy web of factors: economic indicators, consumer sentiment, innovation, regulation, politics, and more. But our brains prefer clarity over chaos. So we take that complexity and boil it down into a simple, clean story with heroes, villains, and a clear cause-and-effect arc. That is why you so often hear things like, "The stock went up because earnings beat expectations," or "The market fell on Fed comments." There may be some truth there, but the full picture is almost always more complicated.

We like stories that make sense. But the danger is that these stories often skip over all the uncertainty, nuance, and randomness involved. They give us the illusion of understanding, which can be just as dangerous as actual ignorance.

Then comes the second part: complexity aversion. Once we have settled on a narrative, we tend to stick with it. Remember the confirmation bias from the previous chapter? New facts get filtered through the lens of the story we have already accepted. Supporting data gets amplified. Contradictions get explained away, ignored, or dismissed. It is not that we do this on purpose. It is just how the human mind works. We look for coherence. We like being right. And once we believe something, we subconsciously protect that belief.

This becomes especially risky in investing. A company might have a great narrative. Maybe it is "disrupting" an industry or "reinventing" something important. But if the fundamentals do not line up, clinging to the story can lead to poor decisions. And on the flip side, we might miss out on solid opportunities just because the story is not exciting or easy to tell.

So narrative bias pulls us in two directions: it oversimplifies a complex world, and then it helps us ignore anything that complicates the picture. That is how we end up favoring investments that sound good rather than ones that actually are good.

The trick is staying aware. When a story feels a little too satisfying, that is often the moment to dig deeper.

BIAS IN ACTION: The Tesla Story Machine

If there is one company that perfectly captures the power of narrative in investing, it is Tesla. More than just a carmaker, Tesla, under Elon Musk's leadership, has built a story machine that is rivaled only by its manufacturing lines. And it is that story, more than the spreadsheets, that has often driven its stock price.

Tesla did not start with a grand master plan. The first story was simple: an electric sports car that did not suck. That was the original

Roadster. Then it morphed into a mission to bring electric vehicles to the masses with the Model S, then the Model 3. From there, the story kept growing: autonomous driving, robotaxis, solar energy, battery storage, even humanoid robots and artificial intelligence. Each new chapter added fuel to the fire, giving investors a fresh reason to believe, even when the financials were shaky.

That makes Tesla such a textbook case in narrative bias. The point is not whether all those visions come true. Many of the Tesla stories actually did come true. The point is how much those visions have shaped the stock's valuation, often far more than earnings or unit sales ever could.

There were times when Tesla was worth more than all other major automakers combined, while selling just a sliver of the cars and posting far smaller profits. Traditional valuation models simply could not explain the price. But the story could. Investors were not just buying a company; they were buying a future, a belief in disruption, innovation, and Elon Musk's ability to bend reality (Steitz, 2020).

And once that belief took hold, a funny thing happened: facts started taking a back seat. Production delays? Just part of the journey. Fierce competition from legacy automakers? Dismissed. Negative cash flow or quality control issues? Overlooked. The narrative became so powerful that any criticism felt like heresy. Tesla bulls and bears stopped debating facts and started defending identities.

In reality, Tesla is both things: a company that has pulled off some incredible technological feats and one that has also stumbled, missed targets, and faced plenty of scrutiny that would have sunk a more "normal" company. But because the story was so strong, it created a kind of emotional buffer. Investors did not just analyze Tesla. They believed in it.

That belief helped Tesla achieve things few companies ever have. But it also shows the risk of narrative-driven investing. When the story is that compelling, it can cloud judgment. You stop asking, "What is it worth today?" and start thinking only about what it might be worth someday.

Tesla is a reminder: stories are powerful. But in investing, the best stories are the ones backed by solid execution.

Categories of Investment Narratives: The Stories We Fall For

Some investment stories show up so often, you could almost set your watch by them. They come dressed in new clothes each time. Different industries, different buzzwords. But the structure is always familiar. These are the crowd-pleasers of the market narrative world, the kinds of stories investors love to believe. And the more you recognize the patterns, the easier it gets to pause and ask: "Is this story telling me something useful, or just making me feel good?"

Disruption Stories: "This Company Will Change Everything"

The disruption story is one of the most tempting narratives in investing today. It usually sounds something like this: "This company is going to change everything." And in the tech era, it has become almost a cliché. Every startup with a slick pitch claims it is about to upend some legacy industry: healthcare, finance, transportation, you name it.

Here is the tricky part: sometimes it is true. Amazon really did reshape retail. Netflix changed the way we consume media. Apple has left its mark on everything from phones to payments. These are the stories that keep the dream alive.

But for every Amazon, there are dozens of wannabes. Companies wave the disruption flag, stir up excitement, and attract investor dollars, but fall flat when it comes time to execute. The narrative skips over the hard stuff: how expensive disruption really is, how entrenched the incumbents can be, how messy regulation can get, and how often even great ideas run into operational roadblocks.

Disruption is not just about having the right idea. It is about flawless timing, relentless execution, and a huge dose of luck. But that does not make a great story. So the narrative often ignores all that, painting a picture of inevitable dominance.

That is where investors get caught. The vision is bold, the founder is persuasive, and the market is massive. It all feels like it is going to work. But too often, the company spends more time selling the story than solving the real-world problems that stand between them and actual disruption.

Disruption can happen, but it is rare, and it is messy.

Turnaround Tales: "New Management Will Fix Everything"

Turnaround stories are one of the market's most tempting traps. A struggling company brings in new leadership, promises a bold new strategy, and paints a picture of revival. It is a classic comeback narrative, and investors love a comeback. The stock is cheap, the potential is big, and the idea of catching the rebound feels like a savvy contrarian move.

But here is the thing: most turnarounds do not actually turn around.

Peter Lynch, who saw more than his share of these pitches, put it bluntly: "Turnarounds seldom turn." And he was right. While the story sounds great, the odds are stacked against it. The issues that land companies in trouble are rarely simple (Lynch, 1989). They are usually deep-rooted: declining demand, outdated products, rising competition, or a business model that no longer fits the times. A new CEO can bring a new tone, but he or she cannot wave a magic wand.

The problem with these narratives is that they tend to understate how hard it is to fix a broken business. They make it sound like a simple matter of cutting costs or refocusing strategy. But true turnarounds take years, require robust execution, and often depend on favorable market conditions, things no management team can fully control.

What often happens is that investors jump in early, expecting a quick rebound. But reality moves slower. The stock stays stuck, the problems linger, and the "new strategy" ends up looking a lot like the old one, just with better PowerPoint slides.

Growth Narratives: "The Expansion Opportunity Is Endless"

Growth stories are some of the most popular and most seductive narratives in the market. They center on a company that is doing well in one area and now promises to scale that success into new markets, new geographies, or new product lines. The pitch is that what has worked once will work again, and again, and again. Revenue will soar, market share will snowball, and today's small win is just the beginning.

It is an appealing story, especially when early results look promising. But these narratives often gloss over the hard reality: growth is rarely linear, and scaling success is far tougher than it looks on paper.

What these stories tend to skip is just how many things have to go right for expansion to work. A company that dominates its niche usually does so for very specific reasons: brand recognition, customer habits, local knowledge, or a particular operational model. When it tries to expand beyond that comfort zone, those advantages often do not travel as well as expected. New markets bring new competition, unfamiliar regulations, different customer tastes, and logistical challenges that can quickly erode the edge the company once had.

The danger of the growth narrative is that it assumes past success automatically translates into future success, just in a bigger arena. But business is not that predictable. What worked in one place might not work in another. And when that gap between story and execution starts to widen, the market can turn fast.

Merger Synergy Stories: "1+1 Will Equal 3"

The story behind most mergers sounds great on paper. You take two companies, put them together, and suddenly you have magic: cost savings, faster growth, and a strategic edge that supposedly makes the high price tag worth it. It is the business world's version of a fairy tale romance.

But here is the reality: most of these fairy tales do not end happily. Study after study shows that big mergers often fall flat. The promised benefits do not show up, and sometimes the deal ends up destroying more value than it creates. The problems are predictable. Mismatched company cultures, paying too much, and wildly optimistic synergy forecasts rarely hold up in the real world.

Remember the AOL-Time Warner disaster that we discussed earlier? That is a textbook example. But I have seen smaller versions of the same story. I once invested in a software company that got acquired with bold promises of integration benefits. Years later, none of those benefits ever showed up.

Now, that does not mean every deal is doomed. Some mergers do work out. Some turnarounds catch fire. Some disruptors really do keep growing. But the key is to recognize the pattern. When you hear the "synergy and strategic value" pitch, it should raise a flag, not to run away immediately, but to dig deeper. These stories often gloss over the messy, complicated parts. That is where your attention should go.

Watch Out When Stock Picking: Red Flags for Narrative-Driven Companies

It is easy to get swept up in a good story, especially when it is dressed in buzzwords and backed by slick investor decks. But in stock picking, you have to be careful when a company's narrative starts sounding too neat, too much like a pitch and not enough like reality. When that happens, it is often a sign that the story is doing the heavy lifting, not the business itself.

One of the clearest red flags is what I call the "shifting story syndrome." This is when a company keeps reinventing its narrative to match whatever theme is currently in fashion with investors. They will talk growth during bull markets, pivot to profitability during downturns, claim innovation when hype is high, or start dropping words like "AI" and "machine learning" the minute those terms start moving stock prices. I once followed a mid-sized software firm that was a poster child for this behavior. In the early 2010s, they were a "cloud-first" company. A few years later, they were suddenly leading the charge in artificial intelligence. Then, as investor sentiment turned more cautious, they began to emphasize operational efficiency and cash flow discipline. The story always sounded compelling, but their actual execution told a different story: inconsistent results, weak margins, and no real moat. It was a company trying to be whatever the market wanted, rather than building something enduring.

Solid businesses do not need to constantly reshape their identity. They might adjust their tactics or improve their operations, but their strategic direction stays clear. They know who they are and where they are going. Narrative-driven companies, on the other hand, often pivot dramatically because they do not have that core stability. The story keeps changing because the fundamentals are not strong enough to support one.

Another cautionary sign is when a company starts to resemble more of a personality cult than a business. These are the firms where the entire investment case seems to revolve around a visionary CEO. Great leaders matter, but when the narrative becomes all about how one genius will figure everything out, you are walking into dangerous territory. First, it overstates how much impact any one person can have in a complex, competitive environment. Second, it makes it harder to objectively analyze the actual business model. Third, it creates what investors call "key-person risk." If the star CEO leaves, gets distracted, or makes a bad bet, the whole house of cards can come down. I have seen investors hang on too long in these situations, not because the numbers made sense, but because they believed in the story of the person at the top. That is not investing. That is faith.

Then there is what I call the "missing metrics phenomenon." This is when a company leads with flattering, non-standard numbers while downplaying traditional financials. Suddenly, the headline is all about "adjusted EBITDA," or user growth, or lifetime customer value. Meanwhile, deeper in the filings, you notice growing losses, shrinking margins, or ballooning share dilution. These alternate metrics might not be wrong, but when they are front and center and the standard metrics are buried, it is often a signal that management is more focused on shaping perception than improving performance. I have seen this play out in everything from tech startups to legacy businesses trying to rebrand themselves as something sexier. When the numbers feel curated to tell a specific story rather than to reflect reality, that is when I start digging harder.

And finally, be skeptical of companies that routinely wave off complexity. Every business faces challenges. It is the nature of the game. But narrative-driven companies tend to downplay these issues, framing them as minor bumps rather than acknowledging deeper problems. When management keeps calling setbacks "execution issues" or blames every shortfall on temporary conditions, they are often trying to protect the storyline. But markets do not run on stories forever. They run on results. And it is in these glossed-over details that the real risks tend to hide.

The bottom line is this: before you buy into a company's narrative, make sure it holds up to scrutiny. Does the story match the financials? Does the competitive edge actually show up in margins and growth, or just in the investor presentation? Are the problems being acknowledged and addressed, or waved away with buzzwords?

Peter Lynch famously said he prefers businesses "so good that an idiot could run them because sooner or later, one will." (Lynch, 1989) The most reliable investments do not need genius storytelling or superstar CEOs. They have clear economics, real advantages, and results that speak for themselves. In a market full of shiny narratives, those are the stories worth backing.

Escaping the Narrative Trap: Practical Strategies

Escaping the pull of a good story is not easy. Narratives are persuasive, especially when they fit what we want to believe. But if you are serious about improving as an investor, you have to build habits that check this bias. Over the years, I have developed a few practical ways to keep myself grounded when the story starts to get ahead of the facts.

The first is what I call the "narrative versus numbers" check. Before I make any serious investment, I split a page in two. On one side, I jot down the story and the qualitative stuff that makes the business seem attractive: the market potential, the leadership, the vision. On the other side, I put the hard data: revenue trends, margin profiles, return on capital, balance sheet strength. When those two columns do not line up, I lean toward the numbers. I once looked into a buzzy software company pitching an "AI-first" transformation. The story was exciting, but the data showed slowing growth and declining margins. That mismatch told me all I needed to know. I passed.

One final trick I use is flipping the story. If I am excited about a turnaround, I force myself to imagine the opposite: that the company is actually spiraling toward failure. What would that look like? What facts would support that view? I tried this with a retail company pushing a digital transformation narrative. When I flipped the story and asked, "What if these investments are hurting the core business?" I noticed the deteriorating store metrics I had initially brushed aside. It did not kill the investment idea, but it gave me a fuller, more balanced picture.

None of these strategies are silver bullets. But they all serve one purpose: to slow down the story and let reality catch up. Narratives are powerful, but they are only helpful when they are rooted in facts. Otherwise, they are just well-told myths. And as investors, we are not in the myth business. We are in the reality business.

Beyond Stock Picking: Narrative Bias in Market Cycles

Narrative bias does not stop at stock picking. It creeps into how we see entire markets, shaping our understanding of cycles, booms, and busts. If you have been investing for a while, you have probably felt this without even realizing it. Those moments when a story becomes so dominant that it feels like truth.

Each era in the market seems to come with its own grand narrative. In the late '90s, it was the "New Economy," the idea that the internet had rewritten the rules and profits no longer mattered. In the mid-2000s, it was "Housing always goes up," a belief that pushed people to stretch into more house than they could afford. Then came the "Fed Put" story in the 2010s, where any market dip was expected to be rescued by central banks. More recently, we have had the "Everything is being disrupted" narrative, where legacy industries were dismissed as dinosaurs and tech startups with little revenue were suddenly valued like they had moats a mile wide.

These stories have something in common: they simplify the world. They turn complex, uncertain environments into neat little scripts. And for a while, they work. When enough people believe a story, they act on it, driving prices, policy, and sentiment in ways that seem to confirm the narrative. That is how bubbles form. The story feeds the behavior, and the behavior reinforces the story.

But reality does not follow a script. It is messier than any narrative. And eventually, it catches up.

I have been caught up in these cycles myself. During the dot-com bubble, I told myself that tech really was different this time. I was not all-in, but I did not exit early either, because the dominant narrative made skepticism feel like missing out. Then, in 2008, I underestimated the severity of the housing crash. I figured the Fed would step in, like it always seemed to. That was the narrative then that the Fed would not let things get too bad. But things got very bad.

What I have learned is that these big stories do not just influence markets. They shape how we interpret the world. When a narrative is strong enough, it becomes invisible. We stop questioning it because everyone seems to agree on it. That is when it is most dangerous.

These days, I try to keep what I call "narrative awareness." I step back and ask: What is the story everyone believes right now? Is it simplifying something that is actually very complicated? Are we ignoring risks because they do not fit the story?

A good warning sign is when people start saying, "This time is different." History rarely repeats, but it often rhymes. When narratives start claiming that the old rules no longer apply, it is time to get cautious. The most seductive stories are the ones that feel like they explain everything. But those are usually the ones that miss the most.

The Power of Anti-Narrative: Finding Opportunity in Story Gaps

Narratives tend to grab the spotlight, but sometimes the best investment opportunities live in the shadows, places where the story is misunderstood, ignored, or entirely missing. If you are willing to look past the headlines and dig into the reality underneath, you will often find value hiding in plain sight. This is the power of what I call anti-narrative investing: spotting the gaps between perception and reality.

Let's start with the overly negative narrative. Every so often, a company runs into trouble. Maybe a failed product launch, a legal issue, or a management blunder, and the story turns sour. That is fair enough. But sometimes, the narrative outlives the problem. It becomes so deeply baked into the market's view that even real improvement goes unnoticed. I remember looking at Mattel, Inc., a toy company that had suffered through a product recall over lead paint and small magnets. It was a serious event, and the market punished it accordingly. But a couple of years later, they had cleaned up the operation, implemented stronger quality controls, and were back to posting healthy profits. Still, the stock lagged. Investors had moved on, stuck in the old story. That gap between reality and perception created a great entry point. As the narrative slowly corrected, the stock re-rated and delivered solid gains.

There is also opportunity in what I would call "narrative absence." Some companies just do not have a story that sells. They are too boring, too complex, or simply not buzzy enough to attract attention. But that lack of attention can be a gift. One of my best-performing investments was. W.W. Grainger, an industrial supply company with no sexy technology, no grand vision, and no CNBC interviews. What it did have was pricing power, sticky customers, and consistent free cash flow. It traded at a discount for years because no one cared to tell its story. That is often the case with these "narrative orphans." Insurance firms, specialty manufacturers, and behind-the-scenes logistics players do not generate excitement, but they do generate returns.

The market's obsession with storytelling can lead to mispricing. When too many people are chasing the same flashy narrative, prices rise beyond reason. When a stock has no narrative or worse, a negative one, the price can fall below reality. That is the imbalance. And that is where value hides.

Howard Marks put it perfectly when he said, "The prettier the story, the more skeptical I become." I have found the same to be true. The investments that made me the most money were not the ones with great stories. They were the ones with good businesses hiding behind messy, ignored, or forgotten ones (Marks, 2011).

So if you want to think differently in this market, do not just chase the stories everyone is telling. Look for the ones they are ignoring or the ones they have already written off. That is where the real opportunities often begin.

The Final Word: Stories Matter, But Reality Decides

Narratives are not the enemy. In fact, they are essential. Stories help us make sense of a chaotic world. They let us frame complex data in a way our brains can handle. Without them, investing would be cold and mechanical. Just a spreadsheet exercise with no context, no meaning, and no motivation to act.

The real danger comes when we stop seeing the story as a tool and start treating it as truth. That is when narratives become blinding. A good story can overshadow hard evidence. It can downplay risks, oversimplify complexity, and make us feel more certain than we should be. We stop asking questions and start rooting for outcomes. The more emotionally attached we become to a narrative, the harder it gets to see when it no longer matches reality.

What makes narrative bias so tricky is that it works silently. We do not notice when a story starts steering our decisions. We are not always aware when we are filtering out facts that do not fit the storyline we have bought into. That is why the real goal is not to get rid of stories, because you cannot, and frankly, you should not. The goal is to build a better relationship with them.

The best investors I have watched over the years are not those who reject stories outright. They are the ones who can use narratives as working hypotheses, not conclusions. They hold them loosely. They understand that no story, no matter how compelling, can capture the full complexity of a business, a market, or an economy. They are constantly asking, "What am I missing?" or "What if the opposite were true?"

And most importantly, they know not to fall in love with their own narrative. That is when you are most at risk. When you have built a story you really want to be true. Maybe because it makes you look smart, or because it fits with your beliefs, or because you have already committed capital. It gets harder to see clearly. You start looking for confirmation instead of contradiction. And that is when mistakes get expensive.

So here is a habit I try to keep: when I am excited about an investment because the story is just so compelling, I hit pause. I ask myself, "What am I not seeing?" I try to map out alternative explanations for the same facts. Maybe the company is not a turnaround. Maybe it is a value trap. Maybe the visionary CEO is more sizzle than steak. Maybe the growth story is built on shaky ground. This does not always change my conclusion, but it keeps me honest.

Being aware of narrative bias will not make investing simple. It will not eliminate risk or uncertainty. But it will help you steer clear of the worst mistakes, the ones that happen when we confuse a great story with a great business.

In the end, the market pays you for being right about reality, not for having the best story. So, appreciate the narrative. Use it. But do not forget: behind every clean, exciting tale, there is a messier truth. And that is the part worth paying attention to.

Chapter Six

Getting Stuck on Your First Impression

When First Impressions Become Traps

BACK IN LATE 2011, JCPenney's board thought they had found their savior. They hired Ron Johnson, the guy who helped turn Apple Stores into retail gold. Wall Street loved it. The stock popped 17% the day the news broke. Here was a man with a winning track record, fresh off building the most profitable stores in the country. If he could do that at Apple, surely he could do the same for JCPenney, right?

Well, not quite.

Johnson came in like a whirlwind. He scrapped coupons and sales: the very things that had kept JCPenney's customers coming back for decades. In their place, he introduced "everyday low prices." He also redesigned the stores, aiming for that clean, high-end feel, and even brought in upscale brands to give the whole place a fresh identity.

But there was one big problem: JCPenney's shoppers weren't Apple customers. They weren't looking for sleek showrooms and boutique vibes. They were bargain hunters. They liked the chase. They enjoyed feeling like they had scored a deal. So, when all of that disappeared, so did the customers. Sales tanked. The stock got cut in half. Johnson was out in less than two years, and JCPenney never really bounced back (Jopson, 2011) (Clifford, 2012) (Loeb, 2013).

What happened? Johnson made a classic mistake. He got anchored.

Anchoring is when you cling too tightly to a familiar idea, usually the first one that worked for you. Johnson was anchored to Apple's model. It had worked brilliantly there, so he assumed it would work anywhere. But he never stopped to ask: What if this isn't the same game?

He even admitted later, "We didn't test it, because we didn't have time." That's not a strategy. That's overconfidence fueled by anchoring bias. He didn't just bring ideas from Apple. He brought assumptions. And they didn't fit (Business, 2013).

Most of us won't run a retail empire. But anchoring trips us up all the same. We get fixated on a stock's old high, or we cling to our first impression of a company's potential. We assume what worked in the past will keep working. And just like Johnson, we stop asking hard questions.

Good investing and good decision-making mean staying open-minded. The world changes. What worked once might not work again. And when we anchor too tightly to a past success or a familiar playbook, we can miss the very signals telling us it's time to pivot.

So, before you double down on that old belief or hang onto a stock because "it used to be a winner," take a step back. Ask yourself if you are anchored to something that no longer fits the world you are in. It might just save you from a costly mistake.

When a Number Becomes a Ball and Chain

One of my more painful investing lessons came with Macy's. I got in thinking I had found a hidden gem. After all, the company owned some serious real estate, none more valuable than its flagship store on 34th Street in Manhattan. That block alone was worth a fortune. I figured even if retail stayed sluggish, the underlying property value would give the stock a solid floor. That was my anchor.

The stock didn't do much at first, then rallied a bit, and I felt validated. But then the broader retail headwinds picked up. E-commerce kept eating away, mall traffic dropped off, and department stores started looking like relics of a past era. Macy's core business was clearly under pressure.

Still, I held on. Not because I liked the direction the business was heading, but because I couldn't shake that anchor: "This company owns real estate that's worth billions. The market just isn't seeing it yet."

But the truth was, even a trophy property in Manhattan couldn't save a retailer that was losing relevance fast. That real estate value might have looked impressive on paper, but it wasn't helping sales, margins, or long-term viability. I clung to that one shining asset as the stock drifted lower, hoping the market would come around.

It didn't. And neither did Macy's. I finally sold at a loss, realizing I had let one appealing detail (one mental anchor) blind me to everything else that was deteriorating. The business had changed. The landscape had changed. But I stayed stuck, holding on to what used to be true, not what was true now.

That experience drove home something important: even a real asset like prime real estate can become a dangerous anchor if it distracts you from the rest of the picture. Investing isn't just about what a company owns. It's about what it earns, and where it's going.

One of the most common traps in investing is that we get fixated on a specific price. Maybe it's what we paid, maybe it's a stock's all-time high, or maybe it's just some round number someone threw out on TV. And that number starts driving our decisions, even when the facts have moved on.

This shows up everywhere. A friend refused to sell his house when the market cooled, because six months earlier, a neighbor sold for more. Never mind that interest rates had gone up and demand had cooled. He was anchored to that old price like it were carved in stone.

Then there's a colleague who had been watching a stock for months, waiting for it to dip back to last year's price. The problem was that the business had actually improved. The higher price was justified. But he couldn't pull the trigger because he was stuck on the old number.

Or another friend who clung to a falling stock because a well-known analyst had once said it would hit $100. That price stuck in his brain, even as earnings cratered and the company missed expectations again and again.

In all these situations, one number (whether it was a past high, a purchase price, or a round number target) became a mental anchor. It stuck in our heads and quietly shaped every decision we made after that. And the strange thing is, those numbers often don't actually matter. The market doesn't care what price you paid. As Peter Lynch put it, "The stock doesn't know you own it [and doesn't care]" (Lynch, 1989).

That's a humbling reminder. Markets move on. Businesses evolve. But anchoring traps us in the past, making it harder to respond to what's right in front of us.

Price is only part of the story. The only number that matters now is what the stock is worth today, based on current realities, not outdated expectations.

Letting go of old anchors isn't easy. But it's one of the most useful skills you can develop as an investor. The sooner you stop looking backward, the clearer your path forward becomes.

Anchoring in Negotiations: Why the First Number Matters So Much

Anchoring isn't just a trap for investors. It's everywhere, especially in negotiations. In fact, some of the most dramatic examples of anchoring happen when two people sit down to haggle over a price.

Plenty of research backs this up: the first number mentioned in a negotiation sets the tone. It becomes a reference point that shapes everything that follows. That's why smart negotiators are often very strategic about who speaks first and what they say (Mussweiler, 2001).

Take mergers and acquisitions. The initial offer a buyer puts on the table almost always sets the range for the final deal. Even if the two sides go back and forth for weeks, that opening bid acts like gravity, pulling the final price toward it. It doesn't matter if it's aggressive or conservative. Once it's out there, it frames the whole conversation.

I've seen the same thing happen over and over in real estate. Two identical houses (same street, same floor plan) can sell for different prices just because of where they were initially listed. A home listed at $495,000 might sell for $485,000. But list the same home at $525,000, and it might go for $510,000. Why? That first number became the anchor. Even when everyone knows it's just a starting point, it still exerts a quiet influence.

Seasoned negotiators know this. That's why they often come in hot with a number that seems extreme. It's not just bluffing. They are setting the terms of the conversation. And more often than not, it works. That first number lodges itself in the other person's mind, and it's tough to shake loose from it.

For investors, this has big implications. Whether it's an IPO price, an early analyst target, or initial guidance from management, those first numbers are sticky. They shape our expectations, sometimes long after they have stopped being relevant.

So, when you are evaluating an investment, ask yourself: Am I thinking clearly, or am I stuck to an old anchor? Awareness is half the battle. Because once you see anchoring for what it is, you can start breaking its grip and make smarter, more grounded decisions.

Why Round Numbers Mess With Our Heads (and Stock Prices)

Ever notice how stocks seem to stall at nice, clean numbers like $10, $50, or $100? There is no real magic in those prices. They do not come from earnings reports or discounted cash flow models. But they still carry weight. That is the anchoring effect in action again, this time with round numbers.

We are wired to use round figures as mental landmarks. They are easy to remember, easy to focus on, and they just feel meaningful, even when they are not. So, when a stock starts creeping up toward $100, a bunch of investors suddenly set that number as a sell target. Others put stop-losses just below it. And like clockwork, the price often hesitates or bounces around at that level.

Once you start noticing this pattern, it shows up everywhere. Traders react to $50 as if it is some kind of cliff or milestone. $99.99 feels like a deal, and $100 feels expensive, even if nothing about the business has changed.

I have learned to use this to my advantage. If I am buying a stock and it is racing toward $100, I do not rush in. I wait to see if it struggles to break through. If I am selling, I do not aim for $100 exactly. I will often set my sell order just below, say at $99.80, because I know plenty of other folks are aiming for that same round number.

It is not about trying to outsmart the market with precision timing. It is about recognizing that everyone, including you and me, is influenced by these subconscious anchors. The trick is to be aware of them and let that awareness shape your game plan without getting caught in the same traps yourself.

Breaking Free from Anchors: Why I Always Use More Than One Yardstick

Anchoring is tricky because it sneaks up on you. You do not even realize it is happening until you are already leaning too hard on one number. Maybe a past stock price, an analyst's target, or something you read on page two of a research report. I have fallen for it more times than I would like to admit.

But there is one method that has helped me break free from that mental grip: I call it the Multiple Anchor Approach. Instead of clinging to one reference point, I deliberately build a few. Think of it as getting several opinions before making a big decision. It forces you to think broader.

Whenever I am looking at a serious investment, I now make myself go through at least three different ways of valuing it. I might start with price-to-earnings, then look at price-to-sales, and finish with a discounted cash flow model. Each one gives me a slightly different angle. None of them is perfect, but together, they paint a more complete picture, and no single number gets to dominate the conversation.

Here is the kicker: I try to do this before I check what the market is pricing in or what analysts are saying. That way, my own work sets the baseline, not someone else's guess. Once you have seen the market price, it is tough to unsee it. It becomes the anchor you start comparing everything to.

Even more important, I regularly scrap old estimates and start fresh. I do not just tweak the numbers. I rebuild the valuation from the ground up. This "zero-based" mindset helps me avoid getting anchored to past assumptions that may no longer apply.

This is not about building perfect models. It is about staying grounded. When you force yourself to use multiple valuation methods and redo them from scratch, you give your brain fewer chances to anchor on the wrong thing. And in investing, avoiding big mistakes often matters more than hitting home runs.

How I Have Learned to Break Free from Anchors

Even after years of investing, I still catch myself falling for anchoring bias. That is why I have built a few habits that help shake me loose when my thinking starts to get stuck. Beyond the Multiple Anchor approach I mentioned earlier, here are a few other strategies that have really helped me think more clearly.

First, I use what I call the Bookend Method. Before I commit to any investment idea, I ask myself two simple questions: What is the best-case scenario? And what is the worst that could happen? By deliberately imagining the extremes, whether everything goes right or everything goes sideways, I give my brain new reference points. That weakens the pull of whatever anchor I was stuck on.

Then there is what I call the Clean Slate Method. Every few months, I go through my portfolio and look at each holding as if I did not own it. I ask, Would I buy this stock today at this price? And if the answer is no, I press further: Then why am I still holding it? It is uncomfortable sometimes, but it is one of the best ways I have found to break away from anchoring to my original cost basis. That price—the one I bought at—is history. What matters is whether the investment still makes sense now.

Another habit that has been surprisingly helpful is gathering multiple viewpoints, especially from people who see the world differently than I do. When I was researching Bitcoin in 2017, I read everything I could from both sides of the fence. I looked at what crypto enthusiasts were saying, but I also dug into critiques from economists, bankers, and traditional analysts. Some of them thought Bitcoin was the future of money. Others thought it was pure speculation. Somewhere in between, I found a more grounded perspective.

That mix of opinions gave me more than one mental anchor. It helped me avoid latching onto the hype or the skepticism. And in a space as volatile as crypto, that kind of balance is invaluable.

The big idea here is simple: do not let your thinking revolve around just one number, one opinion, or one story. The more you force yourself to zoom out, the harder it is for anchoring bias to sneak in and steer you off course.

These are not perfect systems. But they have saved me from some bad decisions and helped me make a few good ones, too.

Breaking Free: Learning to Think Without Anchors

At the end of the day, getting past anchoring bias is not just about using clever tricks. It is about building a mindset, one that is flexible, open, and willing to let go of old ideas when the facts change.

The best investors I know are not the ones with the flashiest models or the most complicated spreadsheets. They are the ones who can look at new information and say, "Okay, maybe I was wrong," without clinging to what they believed yesterday. That kind of mental agility is rare, but it is what separates good decision-makers from stubborn ones.

Warren Buffett gave us a great example of this when he changed his tune on airline stocks. For decades, he avoided the sector like the plague. He even joked that someone should have shot down the Wright brothers to save investors from all the money that would be lost in the skies. Then in 2016, after years of watching the industry consolidate and stabilize, he bought in. Not because his old view was irrational but because he recognized things had changed. And he changed his mind right along with them (Inc., 2016).

That is the kind of thinking I try to cultivate. Not always being right from the start, but being willing to get it right over time. That starts with catching myself in the act, realizing when I am anchored to an old price, an old thesis, or an outdated assumption. From there, I use the tools we have talked about (multiple valuations, clean slates, bookend scenarios) to challenge those anchors and keep my thinking fresh.

It is not easy. None of us likes admitting we were wrong, or giving up on a belief we have carried for years. But investing is not about loyalty to your past self. It is about doing what makes sense now, based on what you know today.

With practice, you get better at it. You start to spot those old anchors before they drag you down. And over time, you become the kind of investor who does not need to be perfect. Just adaptable, open-minded, and willing to evolve.

You've reached the midpoint of *The Psychology of Stock Market Investing*

Thank you for coming this far with me.

Before you dive back in, I just wanted to pause for a moment and ask: if you're finding the book meaningful so far, would you consider leaving a quick, honest review on Amazon? Even a few sentences can help new readers find the story and make a big difference for indie authors like me.

Thank you again for reading and now, on to the rest of the book!

Chapter Seven

Why We Can't Admit We're Wrong

T HERE'S A REASON PEOPLE say it's hard to quit while you're behind. The deeper you're in, the harder it is to walk away, even when it's clearly the smarter move. That's what happened to the U.S. in Vietnam between the mid-1960s and early 1970s. What started as a limited mission kept expanding. Every time things got worse, the response was more troops, more money, more speeches about winning, even when the private reports said otherwise.

By the time the U.S. pulled out in 1973, over 58,000 Americans were dead, and the war had cost hundreds of billions. One of the key architects of that policy, Robert McNamara, later admitted they had been "terribly wrong." But he also said they owed it to future generations to explain why. That "why" isn't just about war or politics. It's a story investors live out all the time, just on a smaller, more personal scale (McNamara, 1995) (Sheehan, 1988).

When you're invested emotionally, financially, or both, it gets harder to change your mind. Instead of cutting losses, people double down. Not because the facts support it, but because admitting a mistake hurts. That's commitment escalation.

Back in late 2012, Bill Ackman made one of the boldest calls of his career. He stood in front of cameras and investors and said Herbalife, a global nutrition company, wasn't just overvalued, it was a pyramid scheme. And he backed that claim the way Ackman often does: with a massive bet. He shorted the stock, reportedly to the tune of $1 billion, expecting the price to collapse to zero.

But instead of folding when the stock held steady and at times even rallied, Ackman dug in. He didn't just place a bet; he launched a campaign. Press conferences. Slide decks. Regulatory lobbying. He even funded investigations to prove his case. The deeper the stock resisted, the deeper his involvement became.

Meanwhile, other big names started piling in on the other side. Most famously, Carl Icahn took a long position and publicly clashed with Ackman, adding more fuel to the fire. The story turned into a public grudge match, part finance and part ego.

And that's where the escalation trap snapped shut. As time dragged on and the thesis failed to play out, Ackman didn't reassess. He recommitted. He'd invested too much. Not just money, but reputation. Backing down would mean admitting he got it wrong in front of the entire investment world.

Years passed. Herbalife didn't collapse. In fact, it proved far more resilient than many expected. By 2018, after enduring years of mounting losses and public battles, Ackman finally closed the position. The bet didn't pay off and the costs, both financial and reputational, were steep (Goldstein, 2012) (Wapner, 2018) (Wang, 2018).

The lesson here isn't about whether Herbalife was ultimately a good or bad company. In fact, the stock has dropped significantly since its 2018 peak, down more than 90% by 2025. But that only reinforces the point: Ackman may have been directionally right. The real problem wasn't the thesis. It was the process.

Instead of staying flexible and letting the facts guide his next move, he got locked into a public battle. His identity became tied to the outcome. And once that happens, it's not just about the investment anymore. It's about winning.

When a thesis becomes a mission, it gets harder to walk away, even when the facts no longer support the fight. Ackman's Herbalife saga is a vivid example of how easy it is, even for the best in the business, to fall into the escalation trap.

And that's what makes it such a powerful cautionary tale. The bigger the stage, the harder it is to fold and the higher the price when you finally do.

The Escalation Trap: Why Letting Go Feels So Hard

If you've ever held onto a losing investment way longer than you should have, you're not alone and you're not crazy. There's a web of psychology working against you, and it's sneakier than you'd think. What starts as a simple investment decision can slowly morph into a mental trap that's hard to escape.

Let's break it down.

First, there's the sunk cost fallacy. This one gets almost everyone at some point. It's the idea that because you've already spent money, time, or energy on something, you feel like you have to see it through, even when the smart move is to walk away. Rationally, those past costs are gone. Spent. They're not coming back, no matter what you do next. But your brain doesn't like that. It tells you, "You've already put so much into this. Don't waste it." (Blumer, 1985)

Now layer on self-justification. This one's about pride. We all want to think of ourselves as smart, capable people who make good decisions. So, when something starts going wrong, instead of admitting the mistake, we build a narrative to protect our ego. "The market just doesn't get it." "This is a long-term play." We find a way to make the decision sound smart, even when it's clearly not working.

Then there's cognitive dissonance. That's the unease you feel when the facts no longer line up with your beliefs. Say you bought a stock because you believed it had a breakthrough drug. Then the data starts looking shaky. You've got two options: admit you were wrong, or twist the facts until they support your original belief.

Guess which one most of us choose?

And finally, we hit loss aversion, which we will discuss in the next chapter. Losses hurt more than gains feel good. That's just how we're wired. So, when you're staring at a red number in your portfolio, your instincts scream, "Do whatever it takes to get back to even." Even if it means ignoring reality. Even if it means risking even more.

That's how people end up doubling down on bad bets. It's not about logic. It's about avoiding pain.

Put all of these together: sunk costs, ego protection, mental gymnastics, and fear of loss, and you get the escalation trap. It's why investors, even smart ones, dig themselves deeper instead of stepping away. What starts as a rational move becomes an emotional commitment. And that emotional commitment turns into a series of increasingly costly decisions.

The tragedy isn't just the financial loss. It's the slow, quiet way your mind tricks you into compounding the mistake. Knowing these forces won't make you immune, but it will help you notice when you're not thinking clearly, and that's often enough to save yourself before things spiral.

The Three-Act Drama of a Bad Investment

Commitment escalation doesn't hit you all at once. It creeps in, step by step. Once you've lived through it, you start to notice the same pattern playing out again and again, like a three-act drama.

It starts with the initial commitment. This is where the journey begins. You find a company that looks promising. Maybe it has strong fundamentals, a product you believe in, or a story that fits your worldview. You do your research, build a thesis, and put some money to work. This stage feels good. It feels rational. You're thinking like an investor, weighing risks and estimating upside. Even if you've missed something, you don't know it yet. And, importantly, your ego isn't fully on the line.

Then comes Act Two: disconfirmation. This is when the story starts to wobble. Maybe earnings miss expectations. Maybe a key product launch gets delayed. Or maybe a competitor comes out of nowhere with something better. You start to see cracks in your original thesis.

Now here's the critical point. This is a fork in the road. You have new information. The honest move is to reassess: Does the thesis still hold up? But that's not easy. The moment your view is challenged, your mind starts scrambling. You feel tension that uncomfortable gap between what you believed and what reality is now suggesting. That's cognitive dissonance.

Which brings us to Act Three: the escalation response. This is where things go off the rails.

Instead of stepping back and re-evaluating with a cool head, we double down. Maybe we buy more shares to lower our cost basis. Or we stretch the story. "This is a long-term play now." We dig for data that supports our case and conveniently ignore what doesn't. We start focusing on side details. A new hire, and a product line. Anything to keep hope alive.

Emotionally, we're in deep now. We've gone from investor to defender. We join message boards, talk ourselves into staying the course, maybe even scoff at the "short-term thinkers" who sold. We don't want to be wrong, and selling would mean we are. So we cling tighter.

And here's the kicker: every round of escalation makes the next one easier. What started as a small, rational two percent position slowly could swell to something much riskier. Not because the company improved, but because we kept trying to avoid the pain of being wrong.

This pattern is incredibly common. But once you know the structure (the clean setup, the moment of challenge, and the dangerous third act), you can start spotting it in real time. The goal isn't to avoid mistakes entirely. It's to catch yourself before a small mistake becomes a big one.

Recognizing the phases gives you a shot at stepping off the treadmill early, before you let a bad decision write the whole story.

BIAS IN ACTION: How GE Got Stuck in the Escalation Trap

It's tempting to think that psychological traps like commitment escalation only trip up individual investors. But they don't stop at our brokerage accounts. They show up in boardrooms too, sometimes with even more costly consequences.

Take General Electric, for example. For decades, GE was one of the crown jewels of American industry. Jack Welch turned it into a management icon, a sprawling conglomerate that seemed to do everything well, from jet engines to light bulbs to financial services.

Then came Jeff Immelt, who took the reins in 2001. What he inherited was a complex beast. GE Capital, the company's financial arm, had grown enormous and risky. But rather than confront those structural risks head-on, Immelt kept the machine running as if nothing had changed.

Instead of acknowledging that GE's business model needed a reset, the company doubled down. They kept paying hefty dividends and buying back shares, even as their industrial units struggled to produce the cash to support those payouts. From 2015 to 2017 alone, GE returned $54 billion to shareholders at a time when it desperately needed that cash to fix the engine under the hood.

It didn't stop there.

GE also went big into oil and gas just before energy prices tanked. When the timing turned sour, they didn't pull back. They went further in, merging their oil business with Baker Hughes in a complicated deal that only made the situation messier. It wasn't a strategy. It was escalation, a refusal to admit that the original plan had gone sideways (Mann, 2020).

Meanwhile, the story kept changing. In one quarter, GE was simplifying. Then it was digitizing. Then it was focusing on services. But underneath the spin, the company was stuck. Stuck in a cycle of trying to salvage past decisions instead of rethinking the future.

And the stock price told the story. It slid from above $30 to below $10. Even as things got worse, GE kept promising that a turnaround was just around the corner. If they could just buy a little more time, spend a little more money, or hold on a little longer.

It wasn't until Immelt stepped down in 2017 that reality finally caught up. The new leadership slashed the dividend, sold off major divisions, and started the painful process of fixing what had long been broken. By then, hundreds of billions of shareholder value had been lost (Egan, 2018).

The GE story is a masterclass in escalation of commitment. The same forces that make it hard for us to sell a losing stock (sunk costs, pride, cognitive dissonance, and the sting of loss) play out just as powerfully at the top of billion-dollar companies. When corporate leaders fall into these traps, the fallout spreads much wider.

And the lesson is the same whether you're managing a $10,000 portfolio or a $100 billion company. If the facts change, your thinking has to change too, no matter how much you've already invested in the old plan.

When Everyone's Watching: How Public Commitment Traps Us

One of the strongest forces behind commitment escalation is something we don't often think about: the pressure of being watched.

It's one thing to make a decision privately and later admit you were wrong. It's a very different thing when that decision was public, and when your reputation, your authority, or your credibility is tied to it. Once we make a choice in front of others, we become more than just financially invested. We become emotionally and socially invested. That makes it a lot harder to backtrack.

You see this all the time in the investment world.

Take fund managers, for example. They often hold on to losing positions much longer than retail investors. Why? Because their moves are public. Clients, colleagues, and even competitors are watching. Selling a loser too quickly can look like admitting they were wrong. In that world, perception matters.

The same goes for CEOs. If a chief executive has gone on record saying a new strategy or acquisition is a game-changer, they're going to have a tough time reversing course, even when the numbers say it's failing. The bigger the public pitch, the harder the climbdown.

Group dynamics can make it worse. Investment committees, for instance, often dig in more than individuals. Once a decision has been discussed, debated, and agreed on in a room full of smart people, there's a natural instinct to stick with it. Nobody wants to be the first to say, "Maybe we got this wrong."

Even market strategists fall into this trap. If you've gone on CNBC and predicted the S&P will hit 5,500 by year-end, there's real pressure to stick to that call, even when the data shifts. Public predictions have a way of turning into personal crusades.

I saw this firsthand in an investment group I used to be part of. One member gave a detailed presentation on a tech stock he believed in. He backed it with charts, financials, and even some glowing customer anecdotes. It was convincing. But over the next year, the company missed on several fronts. Execution slipped, growth slowed, and margins compressed. Still, instead of scaling back, he kept buying more. Eventually, it became his largest position.

In private, he admitted doubts. He wasn't blind to the problems. But having made a public case, he felt stuck. Changing course meant going back to the same group and saying, "I was wrong." That's never easy. So he stayed the course, even though the facts no longer justified it.

That experience taught me something important: public commitment changes the game. It raises the stakes, narrows your flexibility, and makes honest self-correction feel like defeat instead of strength.

Here's the good news. Once you know this, you can build guardrails. Maybe it means keeping some positions private until they've matured. Maybe it means creating space within a team where people can admit mistakes without judgment. Maybe it's as simple as agreeing ahead of time that every thesis will get a review if certain conditions change. That might be an earnings miss, rising debt, or insiders selling.

The key is to give yourself room to pivot. In investing, being right eventually matters more than being consistent publicly. Sometimes, the best decision you'll ever make is saying, "I've changed my mind."

Stock Picking? Keep an Eye Out for the Escalation Red Flags

One thing I've learned over the years is that commitment escalation isn't just a personal bias. It shows up in the companies we invest in, too. If you're not careful, you can get pulled into someone else's blind spot.

Some businesses, especially those led by bold, charismatic CEOs, can look great on the surface but carry serious escalation risk under the hood. That risk tends to show up when management sticks too hard to a strategy that clearly isn't working, just because they've made a public bet on it.

Let's talk about some signs to watch for.

First, beware the personalized strategy. If a CEO is constantly saying "my vision" or "my strategy," rather than "our team" or "our plan," take note. That kind of language might sound inspiring at first, but it usually means the leader sees the business plan as a reflection of themselves. When the plan struggles, they're far less likely to pivot because changing direction feels like personal failure.

Another red flag is unwavering forecasts. If a company keeps repeating the same aggressive targets, even after falling short again and again, that's not confidence. That's delusion. Good managers adjust based on facts. The ones stuck in escalation mode keep promising the moon while shoveling more money into strategies that don't deliver.

Then there's the defensive posture. Watch how management responds to fair questions from analysts or shareholders. When criticism is met with defensiveness or personal attacks, that's a big warning sign. It often signals that the team is more focused on protecting egos than solving problems.

I remember an earnings call where an analyst asked about sagging margins. The CEO didn't address the question. He attacked the analyst, saying he "clearly didn't understand the industry." That kind of reaction doesn't just show thin skin. It suggests an unwillingness to question their own assumptions.

Lastly, beware the forever pivot. Some companies seem to reinvent themselves every few quarters. A new initiative, a fresh brand, a big shift in strategy — all without finishing or acknowledging the last one failed. That's not agility. That's a refusal to admit when something didn't work.

Before putting your money into a business like that, dig a little. See if they've ever publicly owned a mistake. The best companies, the truly durable ones, aren't the ones that never screw up. They're the ones that admit when they have, and fix it early.

One mindset I admire comes from Jeff Bezos: "Be stubborn on vision, flexible on details." That's the sweet spot. Know where you're going, but be willing to change the route when the map changes. When you find a business that operates like that, you're in better hands.

The Final Word: Know When to Fold

Charlie Munger once said that part of learning in life is knowing how to quit, especially when the facts change. He compared it to poker: you have to learn to fold, even when you're holding a hand you once loved. That's not just clever. It's the heart of escaping the escalation trap.

Good poker players don't let their past bets dictate their next move. They focus on probabilities, not pride. Investing works the same way. You have to be willing to let go of a position, even if you've poured time, money, or emotion into it. Even if you once believed in it with everything you had.

The problem isn't being wrong. That's inevitable. Every investor, even the greats, takes hits. The real danger is what happens after the initial mistake, when we refuse to let go. We end up making it worse. That was the hard lesson I learned from one of my previous investments. What started as a two percent position turned into something far costlier, not because the facts were unclear, but because I couldn't bring myself to fold.

The real magic comes when you stop seeing folding as failure. Letting go of a bad investment isn't weakness. It's wisdom. It means you've freed up capital, time, and attention to pursue better ideas. It means you're staying in the game for the long haul.

The key is learning to tell the difference between conviction and stubbornness. One is based on the current odds. The other is chained to the past.

If you can do that... if you can spot the escalation trap early and step off the path, you'll not only protect your capital, but you'll also protect your confidence. And that might be the most valuable asset of all.

In the end, investing well isn't about being perfect. It's about being adaptable. It's about being honest. And above all, it's about knowing when it's time to walk away from a hand that's no longer worth playing.

Chapter Eight

Losses Hurt More Than Gains Delight

Back in 2020, Nikola Corporation was the talk of Wall Street. It had the right story and the right buzzwords: clean energy, hydrogen trucks, and the next Tesla. The company had gone public through a SPAC, and investors couldn't get in fast enough. One institutional investor, someone with a long track record and all the resources in the world, started buying heavily. They were in at prices above $65, confident this was a game-changer.

But in September of that same year, everything started to unravel. Hindenburg Research published a bombshell report accusing Nikola of serious fraud. The most shocking claim? A promotional video showing one of their trucks driving down a road was actually staged. The truck didn't even have a working engine. It was just rolling downhill. That was just the start. The company's claims about its hydrogen tech and upcoming vehicles turned out to be wildly exaggerated.

The fallout was swift. The SEC and DOJ opened investigations. Founder Trevor Milton was eventually charged with securities fraud and sentenced to four years in prison. The stock plunged, down over 40% right after the Hindenburg report, and just kept falling. By mid-2024, it was trading at well below $1 (Justice, 2021) (Research, 2020) (Kolodny, 2020).

Now, here's the part that really sticks with me: that same institutional investor didn't sell. In fact, they bought more and doubled down. From the outside, it looked irrational. The story was broken, the numbers didn't work, and the red flags were everywhere. Why throw more money into a sinking ship?

That's loss aversion at work. The pain of realizing a loss is so intense, we'll do almost anything to avoid it, even if it means risking more money. Instead of admitting the thesis was wrong and cutting their losses, the investor held on. They weren't being stupid. They had access to the best research, smart analysts, and tons of experience. But they were still human.

This isn't just about one investor or one stock. It's a pattern we've seen again and again. In 2008, during the financial crisis, regular investors pulled over $150 billion from equity funds near the bottom. The fear was overwhelming. They couldn't take the red numbers anymore, so they sold and missed the massive recovery that followed.

Loss aversion doesn't care how smart you are. It doesn't care if you've read all the right books. It's baked into how we're wired. Losing feels worse... much worse... than winning feels good. And that imbalance leads to all sorts of bad decisions.

It's one of the great ironies of investing. We build these careful strategies to grow wealth, and then our emotions quietly tear them down. We hold on to losers because selling makes the pain real. We sell winners too early because we're scared of giving the gains back. And in doing so, we chip away at the very compounding we're trying to harness.

That's why understanding loss aversion isn't just helpful. It's essential. Because once you see it clearly, you can start building habits and systems to counteract it. You won't stop feeling the sting of losses, but you'll be less likely to let that sting dictate your decisions. And that's how you stay in the game long enough for your money to actually work for you.

The Everyday Pain of Losing

Loss aversion doesn't just show up in the stock market. It's woven into the small decisions we make every day, often without realizing it.

Take your closet, for example. Have you ever held onto a shirt you haven't worn in years just because you spent good money on it? You know you'll probably never wear it again, but tossing it feels like throwing cash in the trash. That sting? That's loss aversion at work. Logically, freeing up space should feel good. But the pain of "wasting" money you already spent wins the battle.

Or think about that awful movie you stuck with for two hours just because you already sat through the first part. You're not enjoying it. You could leave, change the channel, do literally anything else. But you stay, thinking, "Well, I've already come this far." That's not logic talking. It's your brain trying to protect you from admitting a loss.

Even big life choices aren't immune. A friend of mine told me about a Caribbean vacation she booked months in advance. Just two weeks before the trip, a hurricane was forecasted to hit the island. The hotel offered her an out: cancel now and get 80% of your money back. Sounds like a no-brainer, right?

But she wrestled with it. "I know it's irrational," she said, "but I kept thinking about that 20% I'd lose. Even though if I went, I'd be stuck indoors the whole time, basically losing 100% of the trip."

That's the trick with loss aversion. It doesn't care how smart you are, how much math you do, or how clear the facts are. It grabs you at a gut level, beneath logic. And once it's in the driver's seat, it'll have you chasing sunk costs and making decisions you'd never make if you were starting fresh.

We hate losses more than we like gains. And that simple imbalance runs through everything, from what's hanging in your closet to how you handle your investments. It's not always obvious, but it's almost always there.

How Our Brains React to Losing Money

Neuroscience has finally caught up to what investors have known in their guts for years: losing money doesn't just feel bad. It actually hurts. And it turns out our brains process financial pain in the same places they process fear, disgust, and physical danger.

When we take a financial loss, the amygdala and anterior insula light up. These are old brain structures, hard-wired to keep us alive when threats were lions, not red numbers on a screen. So when your portfolio drops 10%, your brain reacts like you just stepped on a snake. It doesn't know the difference.

Now compare that to a gain. When you make money, the striatum gets involved. That's the brain's reward center, the same place that lights up when you eat chocolate or get a compliment. Gains feel good, sure. But they're smooth and warm. Losses, by contrast, are sharp and cold. They sting. And the sting is much stronger than the sweetness.

The science says the emotional impact of a loss is about twice as powerful as an equivalent gain. Losing $1,000 hits your brain like a punch. Gaining $1,000? It's a pat on the back.

I saw this play out in my own life. I'd put a sizable chunk into a small public company in Korea that looked like the next big thing.

When the stock doubled, I felt satisfied but not euphoric. It was a nice win, but it didn't consume my thoughts.

Then came the crash. That same stock fell more than 50% in just one year. I couldn't stop checking the price. I lost sleep. I'd be in the middle of a meeting or dinner and suddenly catch myself mentally tallying up how much I'd lost. It was a heavy, constant weight.

And that's when you start doing weird things. Behavioral economists have a name for it: the disposition effect. We sell our winners too early and hang onto our losers too long. Why? Because realizing a gain feels nice, and realizing a loss feels awful. So, we grab the sugar early and avoid the pain as long as possible, even if it means hurting ourselves more in the long run.

You've probably felt this. A stock goes up 20%, and the voice in your head says, "Take the win before it disappears." But when it drops 20%? That same voice whispers, "Don't sell now. It's not a real loss unless you sell. It might bounce back."

It's a cruel trick. The brain, trying to protect us, ends up steering us in exactly the wrong direction. We cash out our winners, just as they're gaining momentum, and keep our losers, hoping they'll turn around.

In reality, successful investing often means doing the opposite: letting your winners run and cutting your losers early. But that's not easy when your own brain is fighting you every step of the way.

Why You Can't Stop Checking Your Stocks

There's a reason we keep checking our portfolios, even when we know it's not helping. It's the same reason people pull slot machine levers over and over again: dopamine.

I've got a buddy, Jason, who checks his investment app about 30 times a day. That's not a guess. His phone tracks it. He knows it's excessive, and he's even laughed about it. But he can't seem to stop.

"It's like a reflex," he told me. "I'll be in a meeting at work, and suddenly I'm staring at my phone. I don't even remember pulling it out of my pocket."

What's happening in Jason's brain isn't so different from what happens in a casino. Every time you check and your portfolio is up, your brain gives you a quick dopamine hit. A little jolt of pleasure. Not overwhelming, but just enough to make you want to check again later.

And here's the catch: it's the uncertainty that makes it addictive. Psychologists call it a variable reward schedule. You never know what you're going to see when you open the app. Gains? Losses? A huge rally? Nothing at all? That unpredictability hooks us. It's why slot machines work. It's why we keep refreshing Instagram. And that's why checking your portfolio can become compulsive.

Even when the news is bad, especially when it's bad, you keep checking. You tell yourself, "Maybe this time it'll be different." But most of the time, all you're doing is giving yourself more chances to feel the sting of loss aversion.

This gets dangerous when these two forces, dopamine and fear, collide. The itch to check mixed with the pain of seeing red numbers creates a feedback loop that drives a lot of dumb decisions.

I once knew a retired surgeon who'd spent decades doing all the right things. Lived below his means. Invested in low-cost index funds. Rarely touched his portfolio. He was the poster child for disciplined, long-term investing.

Then he retired. With more free time than he knew what to do with, he started watching CNBC all day and checking his portfolio like it was a Twitter feed. Within six months, he'd flipped into full-time trading mode: buying, selling, and reacting. His annual portfolio turnover jumped from under 10% to over 200%.

When I asked him what changed, he said, "Now I finally have time to take control." But the numbers told another story. His returns had dropped, and his stress had soared. What really happened was simple: dopamine and loss aversion took the wheel.

And there's research to back this up. A study out of UC Berkeley found that investors who got daily updates on their portfolios made 33% less than those who only checked quarterly. Same investments, just fewer check-ins. The difference wasn't strategy. It was emotion. The more often you look, the more losses you see, and the more likely you are to act on fear instead of logic (Thaler, 1995).

It's a good reminder that in investing, more information doesn't always mean better decisions. Sometimes, knowing less and checking less actually leads to more.

It's Not Just About Money

Loss aversion and dopamine-seeking don't just mess with our investing. They show up all over our lives, often in quiet ways we don't even notice.

A few years back, I paid for an annual gym membership. Seemed like a smart move at the time. But after a couple of weeks, I stopped going. Life got busy. Priorities shifted. Still, every month I'd think about canceling, and every month I'd talk myself out of it. "I've already paid," I'd say. "Might as well keep it." That was loss aversion talking. I wasn't getting any value, but the idea of "wasting" the money already spent kept me hanging on.

Then there was a colleague of mine who poured three years into a startup that, frankly, wasn't working. Great idea, solid execution, but the market just wasn't there. When I gently asked if he'd considered moving on, he said, "I've put too much into this to quit now." Again, that's loss aversion. Or more specifically, the sunk cost fallacy. When we invest time or money into something, our instinct is to protect that investment, even when logic says it's time to walk away.

And I'm just as guilty when it comes to dopamine. I'll be in the middle of focused work, trying to write or solve a tough problem, and my hand will go to my phone. No notification, no real reason, just this little itch to check email. Why? Because every so often, there's a fun message, or an unexpected bit of good news. That randomness creates just enough anticipation to keep me hooked.

Once you start seeing these patterns, you realize they're everywhere. Loss aversion and dopamine aren't just finance problems. They're human problems. They shape how we manage time, relationships, careers, and everything.

That's why understanding these two forces is so useful. If you can spot them in your day-to-day life, you can start to spot them in your investment decisions too. And once you see them clearly, you've got a fighting chance at not letting them run the show.

Bias in Action: The Rise of the Smartphone Investor

Something changed when investing moved from desktop screens to smartphones. What used to be a deliberate, occasional process turned into a swipe-and-tap game, accessible anytime and anywhere. And it's had a profound effect on how people behave with their money.

I watched this play out with my friend Jake. For years, he was the kind of investor you'd call steady. He'd log into his brokerage account every now and then, make a trade or two, and then go back to living his life. Nothing fancy, just slow and steady.

Then, in 2019, Jake downloaded a trading app. And everything changed.

"It's just so easy now," he told me. "I can trade while waiting for coffee."

And he did. Within six months, his trading activity had jumped over 400%. He started day-trading options on his lunch break. He'd make snap decisions based on something he saw on Twitter or Reddit. It wasn't investing anymore. It was a reaction. His transaction fees piled up. His tax situation turned into a headache.

And his returns? In a year when the S&P 500 soared over 30%, Jake was up just 12%. And that's before factoring in all those costs.

This isn't just Jake's story. It's happening everywhere. Studies show that investors who switch to mobile trading apps end up trading 67% more. And their returns go down (Vitaly Meursault, 2022). That little dopamine hit from making a trade, the feeling of doing something, feels good. But when combined with loss aversion, it becomes a dangerous cocktail. The more often you check, the more losses you see. The more losses you see, the more you try to fix things with action. And most of the time, that action backfires.

And here's the kicker: the apps are built to do this. They're not just innocent tools. They use the same tricks as social media. Bright colors, confetti animations when you trade. Push notifications that keep pulling you back in. They turn investing into something closer to a video game than a thoughtful process.

Why? Because frequent trading is good for business. These platforms make money when you trade, not when you succeed. Many of them even employ behavioral scientists to make the apps more engaging, which is often code for more addictive.

So, it's not just about having investing at your fingertips. It's about understanding what those fingers are doing and why they're doing it. The convenience is a double-edged sword. If you're not careful, it can turn discipline into impulse and long-term thinking into a series of short-term bets.

Beware of Loss Aversion in the Boardroom

Loss aversion isn't just something that trips up individual investors. It creeps into boardrooms too. And when corporate leaders start making decisions based on pride or past effort instead of present reality, the damage can pile up fast.

Take Walmart's ill-fated expansion into Germany. It had all the makings of a global success story. The biggest retailer in the world entering Europe's biggest economy. What could go wrong?

Turns out, plenty.

German shoppers didn't warm to Walmart's approach. The culture was different, the business model didn't translate, and the competition was fierce. Losses mounted quarter after quarter. It was clear, even early on, that the strategy wasn't working.

But every time the topic came up, management stuck to the same script: "We're turning the corner." "Just one more quarter." There was always a reason to stay the course, even when it was obvious the road ahead wasn't going to get any smoother.

It wasn't until 2006, nearly a decade and about a billion dollars later, that Walmart finally pulled out. When asked why they stayed so long, the answer was painfully familiar: "We had invested so much, it was hard to walk away" (Featherstone, 2006).

That's loss aversion, just playing out on a corporate scale. And it's a costly mindset, not just for Walmart, but for shareholders who watched capital get tied up in a bet that should've been folded long before.

As investors, we have to keep an eye out for these patterns. The same biases that tempt us to hold on to a losing stock show up in how companies manage their operations. Are they still funneling money into failing ventures? Delaying write-downs on assets that clearly aren't worth what they once were? Holding onto legacy divisions that no longer fit, just because they can't admit they missed the mark?

Those are signs that decisions are being driven by emotion, not economics. And if you're putting your money into that business, think twice. Because loss aversion doesn't care if you're a solo investor or a Fortune 500 CEO. It'll wreck long-term returns just the same.

Contrast that with someone like Jeff Bezos, who built Amazon with a ruthless focus on long-term value. He told investors point-blank: "We don't think about the stock price in the short run." That's not just talk. It's a philosophy that allowed Amazon to make big bets, kill off failed projects quickly, and reinvest in what worked (Bezos, 1997).

Warren Buffett puts it even more bluntly: "If you're not willing to own a stock for ten years, don't even think about owning it for ten minutes" (Buffett, 1996). He's not just talking to you. He's talking to the people running the companies you invest in, too.

The best companies (the ones that create real, lasting value) are willing to admit when something isn't working. They take the hit, cut their losses, and move on. Before you invest, take a look at how a company has handled its past failures. Did they cling to bad bets? Or did they reallocate capital like good stewards?

Because in the end, good investing, whether you're buying shares or running a business, means being honest about mistakes, no matter how expensive they feel.

The Enron Lesson: When Denial Turns Dangerous

If you want to see what loss aversion looks like when it goes completely off the rails, just look at Enron.

At first, the story wasn't all that unusual. Some investments weren't panning out. Returns weren't meeting expectations. Nothing fatal, just the kind of bumps any business runs into. But instead of coming clean, Enron's executives tried to paper over the cracks. They couldn't stomach the hit to their stock price or reputation. So, they stretched the truth. A little creative accounting here, a little revenue smoothing there.

But it didn't stop. Each quarter, the pressure grew. What started as bending the rules soon turned into breaking them. They created shell companies to hide losses. They booked future earnings as current profits. Eventually, the whole thing unraveled in one of the biggest corporate frauds in history.

Now, most companies don't end up in handcuffs. But the psychology that started it all (the fear of admitting failure, the refusal to face short-term pain) is surprisingly common in corporate America. And it's why, as investors, we've got to pay close attention not just to what management says, but to how they handle mistakes.

It's easy to praise bold vision and big ideas. But in the long run, what separates great management from mediocre isn't just how they chase growth. It's how they deal with failure. Leaders who can admit when something's not working, take the loss, and move on without ego. That's who you want running your company.

Because at the end of the day, success isn't just about making the right calls. It's about knowing when to stop throwing good money after bad.

The Hidden Cost of Interrupting Compounding

Charlie Munger said it best: "The first rule of compounding is to never interrupt it unnecessarily." It sounds obvious, but when you think about how often we do just that because of fear, boredom, or overconfidence, it hits harder (Munger, 2005).

The thing is, when we let emotions drive our decisions, we're not just messing up a single trade. We're potentially throwing off the entire engine of long-term wealth building. Compounding is quiet, patient, and relentless. But it only works if you let it.

I've seen this play out firsthand. Two friends of mine started investing around the same time. Same age, same income, similar strategies. They both knew what they were doing. This wasn't a case of one person being clueless. But their behavior couldn't have been more different.

One of them checked his portfolio every day. He was always reacting to headlines, tweets, Fed announcements. He traded often, convinced he could outmaneuver the noise. The other barely touched her portfolio. She set a solid plan, checked in quarterly, and almost never made changes.

Fast forward fifteen years. The frequent trader had built up a decent nest egg around $480,000. Not bad by any measure. But his friend? She had over $1.2 million. Same market, same tools, vastly different outcomes.

The difference wasn't luck. It wasn't some brilliant stock pick. It was discipline. Or more specifically, the lack of interruption. The frequent trader paid a price in trading fees, taxes, and, most importantly, mistakes driven by emotion. His friend let compounding do what it does best: work quietly in the background.

That story stuck with me. It's a powerful reminder that building wealth isn't about being the smartest person in the room. It's about giving your investments time to grow without constantly pulling them up to see if they've sprouted.

When you understand how loss aversion and dopamine-seeking behavior play into those interruptions, you can build systems to keep yourself out of your own way. That's the real edge. It's not about chasing more. It's about interrupting less.Top of FormBottom of Form

What Market Crashes Really Reveal About Us

Individual psychology is powerful. When you multiply it across millions of investors, it turns into something even more volatile. That's what we see during every major market crash: a tidal wave of fear and action, driven not by logic but by loss aversion and the deep, almost addictive need to do something.

March 2020 was a perfect case study. As COVID fears spread and markets tumbled, panic set in almost instantly. But what really stood out wasn't just the speed of the drop. It was the behavior. Trading volumes exploded. Investment apps saw usage go through the roof. People who usually never checked their portfolios were suddenly refreshing their screens hourly, trying to make sense of the chaos.

Just like clockwork, many sold near the bottom. They weren't making decisions based on a change in fundamentals or financial goals. They were responding to fear. The pain of seeing losses in real time was too much to bear. In trying to escape that pain, they ended up doing real damage, locking in losses and missing out on the sharp recovery that came just weeks later (FINRA, 2021).

During those weeks, my phone didn't stop buzzing. Friends, family members, acquaintances, and people who hadn't asked me about investing in years were all calling with the same question: Should I sell before it gets worse?

I gave the same answer every time. If your time horizon hasn't changed, why should your strategy?

Most people admitted they still had years, even decades, before they needed the money. But that didn't stop the urge to react. This is the power of mass psychology in moments of stress. It overrides our plans and replaces them with panic.

Looking back, it's clear who came out ahead. The people who held firm, stuck to their plan, and tuned out the noise didn't just recover. They came out stronger. Their portfolios bounced back along with the market. Meanwhile, those who let fear take over often stayed on the sidelines, waiting for the "right time" to reinvest. That time never quite seemed to come.

This isn't new. We saw it in 1929, again in 1987, 2000, 2008, and then 2020. The details are different, but the psychology is always the same. Fear spreads faster than facts. The urge to act and to do something is almost universal. But so is the lesson: staying calm in the face of panic is one of the most valuable traits an investor can have.

What Peace of Mind Really Costs

Sometimes, we knowingly pick investments that don't offer the best returns. It isn't because we don't know better, but because they help us sleep at night. And that's not necessarily wrong. If playing it safe keeps you from panic-selling in a downturn, that's a win. But it's worth being honest about what that peace of mind actually costs.

Let's take a simple example. Historically, stocks have returned around 10 percent a year. Bonds, closer to 5 percent. That 5 percent gap might not look like much over a year or two. But stretch it out over a few decades, and it's a whole different story.

If you invest $10,000 at 5 percent for 30 years, you'll end up with around $43,000. Not bad. But if you invest that same $10,000 at 10 percent, it grows to nearly $175,000. That's a $132,000 difference, all from the same starting amount, just compounded differently over time.

That gap is the price of choosing comfort over growth. For some people, especially those nearing retirement, it might be the right choice. If the volatility of stocks keeps you up at night or tempts you into bad decisions, then paying that price might actually save you money in the long run.

But for younger investors, with time on their side and decades to ride out the bumps, that comfort can come at a steep and unnecessary cost. You're not just trading a few points. You're giving up serious compounding power.

I'm not saying everyone should go all-in on stocks. Far from it. Your investment mix should reflect both your financial goals and your emotional bandwidth. The key is to be clear-eyed about the trade-off. Peace of mind is valuable. Like everything in investing, it has a price. Make sure you're not overpaying for it.

The Final Word: Your Brain vs. the Market

The stock market is the greatest tool ever created for building wealth. At the same time, it is the perfect trap for our worst instincts. It's like putting a caveman in a casino. Our brains were not built for this.

Loss aversion makes us feel a $1,000 loss twice as intensely as a $1,000 gain. It whispers to us to hold on to losing investments too long and to sell winners too soon. Meanwhile, dopamine, our brain's little reward spark, keeps us checking prices, scanning headlines, and refreshing apps like slot machines. Every time we check, we set ourselves up for an emotional reaction. Those reactions, over time, can do real damage.

Together, these two forces can quietly sabotage our long-term returns. Not in a dramatic way, but in a slow, compounding drip of missed opportunities, poor timing, and stress-driven decisions.

But here's the good news. Once you understand what's happening under the hood, you can do something about it. Awareness is the first tool in the toolbox. From there, you can start building systems (automatic rules, scheduled check-ins, portfolio structures) that help protect you from yourself.

Here's the real truth. The biggest threat to your financial future isn't the market. It's not a bad economy or even a bear market. It's you. It's the part of your brain that panics when it sees red, that celebrates too quickly when things go up, and that always wants to act when the smartest move is often to do nothing.

The best investors aren't immune to emotion. They've just learned how to manage it. They build habits and systems that let compounding do its quiet, magical work without unnecessary interruption.

Benjamin Graham said it well: "The investor's chief problem, and even his worst enemy, is likely to be himself" (Graham, 1949).

So, if you take just one thing away, let it be this. Successful investing isn't about being fearless. It's about being self-aware. Know the traps, build your defenses, and stay in the game long enough for compounding to do the heavy lifting.

That, more than any hot stock tip or market forecast, is the real secret to wealth.

Chapter Nine

Following the Herd Into Disaster

B ACK IN JANUARY 2021, the stock market turned into a block-buster movie. And the star? A dusty old video game retailer called GameStop, the kind of place you hadn't thought about since high school. Its stock had been limping along, stuck at $17, while most investors figured it was just another casualty of the internet age. But then, out of nowhere, it caught fire.

And I don't mean a slow burn. I mean explosive. In just a few weeks, GameStop rocketed to nearly $500 a share. Not because it had a genius turnaround plan. Not because profits were soaring. But because an army of retail traders on a Reddit forum called WallStreet-Bets launched a crusade.

It started as a joke, a kind of internet prank on Wall Street. But it snowballed into something much bigger, a full-blown movement. These traders weren't just buying stock. They were buying a story.

They saw themselves as the underdogs, taking on hedge funds that had heavily shorted the company. This was David versus Goliath, with smartphones and memes instead of slingshots.

People jumped in for all kinds of reasons. Some wanted to stick it to the suits. Others just wanted to get rich quick. Many admitted they didn't really understand what they were buying. They just didn't want to miss the rocket ship. For a few euphoric days, it felt like the little guy was winning. Some early birds walked away millionaires. The rest of us watched in disbelief.

Then, just like that, the music stopped.

Trading platforms started freezing purchases. The hype started to fade. The price, once climbing like a rollercoaster, came crashing back down. Hard. A lot of latecomers got caught holding the bag. Some had emptied their savings. Others had borrowed money. All they were left with was regret and Reddit screenshots (Kochkodin, 2021) (Kate Kelly, 2021).

What happened with GameStop wasn't just a financial oddity. It was a living, breathing lesson in crowd psychology. When a story feels good enough, and enough people believe in it, logic takes a back seat. Fundamentals? Who cares? Momentum becomes everything. It was a perfect storm of hype, herd mentality, and a generation of investors learning in real time just how wild markets can get when emotion takes the wheel.

Ever seen a bonfire? It burns bright and fast. That was GameStop.

The Magnetic Pull of the Crowd

The crowd has a strange power. You feel it in a stadium, at a concert, even standing in line when you're not quite sure what for. But if enough people are doing it, part of you just wants to go along. That instinct goes way back. Thousands of years ago, if your tribe suddenly took off running, your best move wasn't to stop and ask questions. It was to run too. That behavior kept your ancestors alive. The ones who paused to analyze got eaten.

That ancient wiring still lives within us today, but now we're not running from predators. We're chasing profits. In the stock market, that old instinct can get us into serious trouble.

I saw it up close in the late '90s during the dot-com bubble. It was a gold rush. Suddenly, everyone was an internet stock expert: barbers, cousins, people who'd never read a balance sheet in their lives. If a company had ".com" in its name, it didn't need profits or even a real product. The stock would soar just on hype.

You'd hear stories everywhere. Friends doubling their money in a month and IPOs tripling before lunch. CNBC was basically throwing a party every day. The fear of missing out was off the charts. If you weren't in tech stocks, you felt like a fool watching everyone else get rich.

Even Buffett, the most disciplined investor of our time, got mocked for sitting it out. People said he didn't understand the "new economy." Those are dangerous words in investing, and history shows they usually precede a crash.

Sure enough, the bubble popped in March 2000. Over the next two years, the NASDAQ plunged nearly 80 percent. Companies that had once been Wall Street darlings, some worth billions on paper, vanished like smoke. A lot of regular investors, the ones who followed the crowd late into the mania, lost everything.

But here's the thing. Those who stayed grounded, who didn't buy into the frenzy, came out ahead. They had cash when everyone else was panicking. They bought real businesses at bargain prices while others were licking their wounds.

The crowd feels safest when it's most dangerous. That's the paradox. When everyone's all-in, when everyone agrees, it usually means all the upside is already priced in. The trick isn't just to think independently. It's to have the courage to act on that thinking when it feels most uncomfortable. That's where the real money gets made.

The Two Faces of the Herd

Herd mentality wears two faces in the world of investing, and both can quietly mess with your decisions if you're not paying attention: external herding and internal herding. Understanding both is crucial for protecting your portfolio from their influence.

External herding is what happens when we start taking our investment cues from the crowd instead of from our own homework. It's that feeling you get when you see a stock shooting up and think, "What am I missing?" Suddenly, it doesn't matter that the numbers don't add up or that you've never even heard of the company until yesterday. The fact that everyone else seems to be in is enough to make you question your own judgment.

There's a name for this: an information cascade. It's when people pile into something not because they've done deep research, but because they assume the earlier folks must have seen something valuable. You start thinking, "If all these people are buying, surely they know something I don't." So, you follow along. But here's the trap. Sometimes, they don't know anything either. They're just copying the person before them (Sushil Bikhchandani, 1992).

I saw this play out in real time during the crypto boom of 2017. Bitcoin, Ethereum. Everything was soaring. People weren't buying because they understood blockchain or had studied the tech. They were buying because prices were rising fast, and their cousin, barber, or college roommate was suddenly making a killing. It was less about investing and more about not wanting to be left out.

Then 2018 hit, and reality checked in. Bitcoin dropped more than 80 percent from its peak. Many of the latecomers who jumped in near the top saw their savings evaporate in a matter of months. Most of them bailed out, shaken, disillusioned, and vowing never to touch crypto again.

Ironically, Bitcoin eventually recovered. In the years that followed, it not only rebounded but hit new all-time highs. Yet many of those early panic sellers didn't stick around to enjoy the comeback. They got caught in the emotional whiplash of herd behavior, rushing in when it felt safe and bailing out when they needed to hold on. That's the cost of following the crowd instead of following a plan.

Then there's FOMO, the Fear Of Missing Out. That's what really juices bubbles. It's not just the greed of wanting to make money. It's the pain of watching others make money while you sit on the sidelines. It makes you ignore risks. You start to think the only thing worse than losing money is not being part of the win.

Look at Tesla between 2019 and 2021. The stock exploded from about $50 to over $1,200. Early skeptics who believed it was over-valued began changing their tune, not because the fundamentals changed overnight, but because the rise felt unstoppable. Many jumped in near the peak, not out of conviction, but out of fear: fear of being the only one who missed the boat.

And finally, there's the warm, fuzzy lie of safety in numbers. It's the logic that says, "Even if this goes wrong, I won't be alone." That mindset led to disaster in 2008. Big banks made terrible bets on subprime mortgages, and when things unraveled, many executives defended themselves by saying, "Everyone else was doing it too." Somehow, being wrong in a crowd felt more acceptable than being cautious and standing alone.

That's the danger of external herding. It tricks us into mistaking popularity for wisdom. But in investing, the crowd often gets loudest right before things fall apart.

Internal herding is sneakier than its loud, market-driven cousin. It doesn't come from CNBC headlines or Reddit frenzies. It happens quietly, in your own bubble. It's when your circle (your news feeds, your favorite experts, your group chats) starts echoing your views back to you. And without realizing it, you stop hearing anything that might challenge your thinking.

Take crypto in 2020 and 2021. Bitcoin was on a tear, and if you were even mildly bullish, chances are you followed people who felt the same. Twitter feeds full of laser eyes. Reddit threads trashing any mention of risk. Newsletters cheerleading every price spike. Before long, every voice in your world was saying the same thing: "It's going to the moon." If someone dared to raise a concern, they were accused of spreading FUD (fear, uncertainty, and doubt). Balanced thinking went out the window.

That's a dangerous combination of confirmation bias and herd mentality.

But it doesn't just happen online. Groupthink can creep into real-world investment teams too. Whether it's a boardroom, a committee, or just a few buddies talking stocks, people naturally avoid being the odd one out. Nobody wants to be a buzzkill. So, when the group leans a certain way, dissent starts to vanish. Sometimes it's subtle, like an approving nod when someone agrees. Other times it's direct: "We all see the upside here, right?" That need for harmony pushes groups into decisions that individuals might avoid on their own. It's called the risky shift, and it's a real thing. Studies show that groups often end up taking bigger risks because everyone assumes someone else has thought through the downside (Stoner, 1961) (Zavalloni, 1969).

Then there's the expert trap. When someone with credentials or a big name gives an opinion, we tend to take it at face value. If a billionaire investor or a bank CEO says a stock is a sure thing, people rush in. Not because they've done their own digging, but because they figure, "If they're saying it, it must be true." That shortcut can work, but only until it doesn't.

In 2007, plenty of smart people ignored the red flags in housing because high-profile experts said everything was fine. "Subprime is contained," they promised. "Housing prices can't fall nationwide." We now know how that ended.

Internal herding is dangerous because it feels like thinking for yourself, but it's not. It's just a quieter version of following the crowd. In investing, echo chambers don't just confirm your beliefs. They amplify them until it's too late to hear the warning signs.

The Digital Amplifier

Technology has always changed how we invest, but in the past decade, it's thrown gasoline on the fire of herd behavior. What used to spread through word of mouth or a weekend newspaper column now travels across the globe in seconds.

Social media platforms have turned markets into high-speed echo chambers. One tweet from Elon Musk can send a stock soaring or crashing. A Reddit thread can rally millions of people behind a struggling company like GameStop or AMC, pushing the stock up thousands of percent with no change in fundamentals. What's changed is speed. The faster information moves, the faster emotions catch fire. When investing starts to move at the speed of a viral video, rational thinking tends to get left behind.

Online forums and platforms can be great equalizers. They've opened up access to financial ideas, tools, and debates that used to be behind paywalls or locked in Wall Street boardrooms. But they can also amplify noise just as easily as signal. One minute you're reading thoughtful analysis, the next you're knee-deep in a hype storm, surrounded by speculation dressed up as certainty. Once enough people start buying based on momentum, it stops being analysis and starts becoming a stampede.

The barriers to joining that stampede are practically gone. With commission-free trading and fractional shares, it's easier than ever to act on a whim. Platforms like Robinhood removed the cost friction that used to make us think twice. Now, someone can see a flashy TikTok stock tip, tap a few buttons, and be in the market before they've even finished their coffee. No fees, no filters, no pause.

This isn't all bad. More people investing is a good thing. More access means more opportunity. But it also means the herd can form faster, move quicker, and grow louder. In this new landscape, emotion doesn't just influence the market. It drives it, sometimes more than logic or value ever could.

This is the new market reality. The tools have changed, but the human impulses (greed, fear, the need to belong) are still running the show. Just faster now.

When Following the Crowd Makes Sense

Here's the catch. Herding isn't always irrational. The truth is that most of the time, especially in large-cap stocks, the market gets it right. Prices in these stocks reflect the collective judgment of millions of investors, including professionals with deep knowledge, powerful tools, and access to information you'll probably never see. Fighting that consensus without a real edge isn't contrarian. It's just overconfident.

If you're a part-time investor, sitting at your kitchen table after work and trying to analyze a semiconductor stock or a biotech start-up, the odds are that the market knows more than you do. Not because you aren't smart, but because the other side of that trade might be a portfolio manager with thirty years of sector experience and a team of PhDs. In these cases, the price isn't noise. It's a signal. Often it's the result of deep, informed analysis that you may not have the time or resources to replicate.

That's where humility comes in. When you're operating outside your circle of competence, leaning on the market's collective wisdom isn't a weakness. It's smart. This is exactly why low-cost index funds are such a powerful tool for most investors. They let you "follow the crowd" in a disciplined, efficient way, without trying to outsmart it. You're buying the average outcome of thousands of well-researched decisions, which over time tends to beat most people's best guesses.

And sometimes, yes, the market is reacting to real, structural change, not just hype. Amazon looked expensive for years, but it kept growing and executing. Apple wasn't just selling gadgets. It was building an ecosystem that reshaped entire industries. The market recognized that, and the prices reflected it. The crowd wasn't wrong. They were early to something big.

The key is knowing when the consensus is grounded in fundamentals and when it's being driven by emotion. That's hard in real time. You can't just look at price movement. You have to dig deeper. Look at the business model, the numbers, and the story underneath. Is this a strong company with staying power, or a narrative stock with nothing behind it?

Following the crowd isn't a mistake if you understand why the crowd is moving. The mistake is assuming the crowd is always wrong and you're always right. Most of the time, the market reflects something close to the truth. It's in the times when it doesn't, when prices disconnect from reality, that you need the courage to act. But don't make the mistake of thinking every consensus is a bubble. Sometimes, the wisdom of the crowd is just that. Wisdom.

Watch Out When Stock Picking

When you're digging into individual companies, trying to separate the winners from the flash-in-the-pan fads, it's crucial to stay on guard for signs that the herd has taken over. When too many people are facing the same direction, they usually stop looking where they're going.

Start with analyst ratings. If every Wall Street report is glowing and the consensus is a unanimous "strong buy," that's not a green light. It's a warning sign. This kind of total agreement tends to show up when optimism is at its peak and all the good news is already baked into the price. History shows that stocks with the most bullish analyst coverage often underperform in the long run. Why? Because when everyone agrees, nobody's thinking critically. Just ask the folks who backed Blockbuster in the early 2000s. Analysts loved it. Cash flow was strong. Stores were everywhere. It looked unstoppable. Netflix was barely a blip on the radar. By the time people realized what was happening, it was too late. Blockbuster was done.

When the media starts treating a CEO like a rock star, plastering them on magazine covers and hailing them as the next Steve Jobs, it's often time to take a step back and think twice. That kind of adoration doesn't always come from substance. Sometimes it's just the market echoing its own excitement.

Take Enron, for example. In early 2001, Fortune named it the "Most Innovative Company in America" for the sixth year in a row. Analysts were dazzled. Investors couldn't get enough. Enron was supposedly reinventing energy and even branching into broadband. It all sounded revolutionary. The stock was flying high, and its executives were treated like business royalty.

But behind the curtain, things were rotten. By the fall, Enron admitted to cooking its books. Massive debts were hidden through off-the-books entities, and profits were inflated or didn't exist at all. By December, it filed for bankruptcy. The media praise had peaked just months before one of the biggest corporate implosions in history (Elkind, 2003).

This isn't a one-off story. Time and again, the market and media fall in love with a company or a charismatic leader, and that love blinds them to the cracks beneath the surface. When you start seeing headlines instead of hard questions, that's usually when risk is highest.

So, when the spotlight is at its brightest, that's your cue to dig deeper. The moment a company becomes too beloved to fail, that's often when it's most vulnerable.

You'll also want to watch for industry bandwagons. When companies across different sectors all start chasing the same trend (whether it's blockchain, the metaverse, AI, or whatever's hot that week), it's usually more about marketing than substance. Remember Long Island Iced Tea? They changed their name to Long Blockchain in 2017, saw their stock triple overnight, and had absolutely nothing to do with blockchain. It was all sizzle, no steak. They were eventually booted from the Nasdaq (Cheng, 2017).

Another big red flag is when people start dismissing traditional valuation metrics. When you hear, "This time it's different," you should start getting very cautious. That line has shown up in every major bubble, from dot-com to housing to crypto. It's a classic way of justifying prices that don't make sense. During the housing boom, people swore real estate always goes up. During the crypto craze, people claimed P/E ratios didn't matter anymore. *Spoiler: they do.*

And don't ignore the shoeshine signals. If your Uber driver, your barber, or your cousin who's never read a 10-K starts giving stock tips, take a step back. That's not arrogance. That's pattern recognition. Bernard Baruch said he sold everything before the 1929 crash when his shoeshine boy started talking about stocks. When investing becomes a party and everyone's invited, the punch bowl is usually about to be taken away.

Finally, watch what companies do, not just what they say. If a company is spending more time trying to goose its stock price than actually building value, that's a red flag. Rushed acquisitions, weird accounting tweaks, or an obsession with quarterly earnings over long-term strategy. These are signs they're playing to Wall Street, not to durable business growth.

Breaking Free from the Herd and Turning It to Your Advantage

The best investors don't just resist the crowd. They make money off their mistakes. They understand that markets are driven by emotion as much as by logic. When fear or greed pushes prices away from reality, they see it for what it is: an opportunity.

Buffett's advice still rings true: "Be fearful when others are greedy, and greedy when others are fearful." (Buffett, 1986) When everyone's piling into the same trade, sometimes the smartest move is to quietly walk the other way.

Look at Buffett during the 2008 financial crisis. While the world was panicking, he was writing massive checks. Everyone else was racing for the exits, but Buffett was buying front-row seats. He put $5 billion into Goldman Sachs with warrants that eventually netted over $3 billion in profit. He scooped up $3 billion worth of General Electric preferred stock with a 10% dividend. And he bought Burlington Northern Santa Fe, betting on the long-term strength of American railroads at a price that turned out to be a steal (Sorkin, 2008) (Roumeliotis, 2013).

Buffett didn't do this because he thought the headlines were going to get better. In fact, he said just the opposite: "The leaks are now turning into a gusher... and headlines will continue to be scary." But that's exactly why he acted. He knew that when fear dominates the market, prices often detach from reality. For someone with cash, patience, and a clear head, that's a dream setup.

It wasn't his first time, either. Back in 1974, when the Dow had dropped nearly 45%, Buffett told Forbes, "Now is the time to invest and get rich." Everyone else was focused on inflation, recession, and oil shocks. He was focused on value and he was right (Magazine, 1974).

The same thing happened in March 2020. COVID hit, the world shut down, and stocks crashed. While most investors were rushing to cash, Howard Marks of Oaktree Capital started buying aggressively. His reasoning was simple: forced selling creates opportunity. If someone has to sell regardless of price, that's when value investors step in.

Howard Marks, another legend in the value investing world, summed it up perfectly: "The greatest challenge for investors is... not letting the mood swings of others infect you." That's the core of the contrarian mindset. It's not about being difficult or disagreeable for the sake of it. It's about recognizing when the crowd has lost its grip on reality and having the discipline to act when it feels most uncomfortable (Marks, 2011).

You don't need to be Buffett or Marks to do this. But you do need a system. A way to stay calm when others aren't. A plan for what to buy when prices drop. And the patience to wait until the panic sets in.

Lessons from the Greatest Contrarians

The best contrarian investors — those rare folks who thrive when everyone else is panicking — tend to share a certain temperament. It's not just about spotting mispricings or zigging when the market zags. It's about mindset, patience, discipline, and the ability to sit still while others are fidgeting.

Start with patience. Contrarian investing doesn't pay off overnight. You're often early. You buy when something looks broken, and it might stay broken for a while. John Neff, who managed the Windsor Fund and beat the market by an average of 3% per year for over three decades, put it best: "It's not always easy to do what's not popular, but that's where you make your money." He bought stocks that looked bad to casual investors but held on until the market caught up to the real story (Mintz, 1999).

Then there's emotional control. If you're going to be a contrarian, you can't ride the emotional rollercoaster that sweeps through the market every time the Fed says something or a chart breaks a line. David Dreman, one of the early voices in contrarian investing, once said, "Psychological factors are even more important than information in the investment process." In other words, how you feel during market chaos often matters more than what you know.

Another trait is that contrarians don't care much about benchmarks in the short term. True contrarians are focused on absolute returns. They're okay underperforming when markets are flying high because they know they'll outperform when things go south. They measure their success over full cycles, not over a hot quarter or a strong year. That kind of long-term focus is a rare muscle, and it's worth building.

And finally, the best contrarians never stop learning. They treat market history like a living textbook. Not because it repeats perfectly, but because it rhymes. Howard Marks, who's known for his clear-eyed memos and deep understanding of market psychology, puts it like this: "Experience is what you got when you didn't get what you wanted." Every mistake becomes a lesson. Every cycle becomes a reference point.

If you want to think like a successful contrarian, it's not about being the smartest person in the room. It's about being the most patient, the most grounded, and the most curious. That's the real edge, and it's one you can build.

Conclusion: The Courage to Think Differently

Herd mentality is one of the most enduring and influential forces in the market. It builds booms, fuels busts, and tugs at even the steadiest hands. It's not just a problem for the inexperienced. It tests everyone, from new investors to seasoned professionals.

But here's the truth: the investors who achieve extraordinary long-term results aren't the ones who best ride the wave of current trends. They're the ones who manage to stay grounded while the crowd gets swept up in emotion. They think independently, not to be contrarian for its own sake, but because they have the discipline and framework to recognize when prices no longer reflect reality.

Every investment decision presents a fork in the road. You can follow the mood of the moment, or you can step back and do the tougher work: digging into the numbers, questioning the story, and thinking for yourself. Most people don't take that harder path, because it's lonely and uncomfortable. Sometimes it means watching your thesis go underwater while the market celebrates something you think makes no sense. Sometimes it means being early and staying patient.

Over time, that mindset is what separates the good from the great. Not raw intelligence. Not flashy trades. Just temperament. As Warren Buffett has said, "The most important quality for an investor is temperament, not intellect." That means staying calm when others panic, holding firm when you've done the work, and being flexible enough to change your mind when new evidence demands it.

The crowd will always be there. It will always have a strong opinion. Your job isn't to ignore it completely, because that's unrealistic. Your job is to be aware of its pull, and to choose when to follow and when to break away. That awareness, combined with curiosity, humility, and a strong internal compass, is what gives you a lasting edge.

In a market driven by emotion, the rarest skill is still clear thinking. And the investors who master it are the ones who build real wealth, quietly and consistently, far from the noise of the herd.

Chapter Ten

Assuming Recent Events Predict the Future

When Yesterday's Winners Become Tomorrow's Laggards

IN EARLY 2021, BILL Hwang looked like a genius. He had turned a sleepy family office called Archegos Capital into a hidden giant on Wall Street. Most people had never heard his name, but behind the scenes, he controlled over $100 billion worth of stock. That is billion with a "B." He started with about $200 million and, in just a few short years, rode it all the way to the stratosphere. His personal fortune was over $10 billion, at least on paper.

The magic trick? Extreme leverage and a very strong belief in momentum. He used a financial sleight of hand called total return swaps, basically secret side deals with big banks like Credit Suisse and Nomura that let him borrow to the moon. With these tools, Hwang could bet five to eight times more money than he actually had. It was like walking into a casino with a hundred bucks and playing at the high-stakes table as if you had a thousand.

He didn't chase just any stocks. He went after the winners. If ViacomCBS was flying, he bought more. If Chinese tech stocks were hot, he went all in. Every time these stocks climbed, he felt validated. It wasn't just confidence. It was euphoria. The more he won, the more he bet. He believed he had cracked the code: find what's going up and ride it.

But leverage works like gasoline. It makes everything faster, both your gains and your losses. The unraveling started quietly enough. On March 22, 2021, ViacomCBS announced a $3 billion stock offering. This was a company whose shares had nearly tripled since the start of the year. So when management suddenly decided to issue more stock, investors took it as a red flag. It looked like the insiders thought that the price had gotten ahead of itself and that the stock was too expensive.

The market didn't take it well. The next day, the stock slid 9 percent. Then, on March 24, it fell off a cliff, dropping another 23 percent. For most investors, that kind of move is painful. But for Bill Hwang, whose fund was built on extreme leverage and concentrated positions, it was catastrophic. ViacomCBS wasn't just any holding.

It was one of Archegos' biggest bets. This wasn't a case of normal market noise. The plunge was sharp and specific, and it lit the fuse. Banks called in their margin. Hwang couldn't cover it. That is when everything started to crumble.

What happened next was a fire sale unlike anything seen in decades. Stocks got dumped at lightning speed. Other banks panicked and raced to offload their shares before they too got burned. The sell-off fed on itself like a stampede. When the dust cleared, Archegos was gone. Hwang's $10 billion fortune was vaporized. Credit Suisse alone lost $5.5 billion and was acquired by UBS in March 2023 in a government-brokered rescue, with the Archegos loss being one of several factors that contributed to its eventual demise (Katherine Burton, 2021) (Juliet Chung, 2021) (Ashworth, 2021) (Maureen Farrell, 2021) (Gregory Zuckerman, 2021).

This wasn't just a story about greed or bad risk management. It was recency bias in its purest, most dangerous form — the belief that the recent past is a reliable map for the future. Hwang bet the farm on the idea that what had been working would keep working. And he didn't just bet the farm. He mortgaged the farm five times over.

We all do this in our own way. When tech stocks are soaring, we think they will keep soaring. When real estate keeps going up, we believe it is a one-way street. Our brains draw straight lines from what just happened and extend them out forever. It feels smart, like we are learning from experience. But more often than not, it is a trap.

Markets don't move in straight lines for long. Leadership rotates. Trends reverse. The crowd favorite of yesterday becomes the dud of tomorrow. History is full of examples.

After the dot-com crash in 2000, value stocks led for nearly a decade. Then, from 2007 to 2020, growth stocks took over and made heroes out of anyone who held big tech. In 2022, the pendulum swung again. It is the same story with U.S. versus international stocks. In the 2000s, international beat U.S. hands down. But starting in 2008, U.S. stocks crushed global returns. Now, after years of underperformance, international stocks might be primed for a comeback. Small caps, large caps, bonds. It all goes in cycles.

Here is where it hurts: we often chase the last winning strategy and dump the stuff that is out of favor. That means buying high and selling low. Morningstar studied this and found that investors underperform the very funds they invest in by 1.7 percent a year just from poor timing. Over decades, that small gap snowballs into a massive hit to your wealth (Kinnel, 2020).

Good investing does not require a crystal ball, but it does demand humility and patience. Sometimes the best move is to sit tight with the boring stuff, because today's underperformer could be tomorrow's star. Recency bias tricks us into ditching diversification, which is the only true free lunch in investing. Slowly and silently, that is how long-term returns get eaten away.

Bill Hwang's rise and fall is a cautionary tale, not just about leverage, but about the seductive pull of recent success. When you start believing the party will never end, that is usually the time the music stops.

The Trap of Extrapolation

One of the most common mistakes investors make is projecting the recent past into the future. It shows up as simple trend extrapolation, assuming whatever just happened in the market is going to keep happening indefinitely.

We do it in both directions. When markets are falling, we assume the decline will continue. When they are rising, we assume the gains will never stop.

You could see this play out in real time during the COVID crash in March 2020. As the market plummeted more than 30 percent in just a few weeks, people were bracing for the worst. My inbox filled with dire warnings, not from fringe corners of the internet, but from analysts, advisors, and friends.

"The market could fall another 50 percent from here." "This is just the beginning of a multi-year bear market." "We might be heading into a depression."

None of these forecasts was based on detailed analysis of stimulus plans, interest rates, or virus containment. They were emotional reactions to what had just happened. If the market could fall 35 percent in a month, why not 35 percent more?

But then came the snapback. The market staged one of the fastest recoveries in history, leaving many doomsayers stuck on the sidelines. Even as the real-world pain of the pandemic played out, markets began pricing in stimulus, adaptation, and eventual recovery.

And it works the same way on the upside. Fast forward to 2021, and those same voices that predicted doom were suddenly talking like stocks could only go up. We saw speculative bubbles in crypto, meme stocks, and even traditional sectors. "Buy the dip" turned into "buy anything," and people stopped asking whether gains were sustainable. They just assumed the good times would keep rolling.

This behavior is not just about overconfidence or fear. It is how our brains are wired. Psychologists call it availability bias. We give more weight to what is right in front of us, especially vivid, emotional events, than to long-term patterns or history books. A recent market crash feels more "real" than a crash you have only read about. A hot run of gains feels like a permanent new normal.

The key is recognizing this tendency before it shapes your decisions. Because investing is not about predicting what just happened. It is about preparing for what could happen next. And in markets, the future rarely looks like the immediate past.

The Base Rate Blind Spot

One of the sneakiest ways recency bias trips us up is by pushing us to ignore base rates, the long-term probabilities that should guide our expectations. Instead, we fixate on what has happened lately and assume it will keep happening.

Picture this: historically, U.S. markets experience a bear market, a drop of 20 percent or more, about every 3.6 years. Now imagine we are five years into a bull run, and the market is hitting new highs every month. What does the recency bias do? It tells us the good times will roll on. After all, stocks have been rising for years. Why stop now?

But the base rate tells a different story. We are overdue. Not guaranteed to crash tomorrow, but statistically, a downturn becomes more likely with every month of uninterrupted gains. Ignoring that is like driving full speed through a yellow light just because the last few stayed green.

This disconnect was front and center in late 2007. Markets had recovered beautifully from the dot-com bust. Real estate was booming. Risk felt like a thing of the past. But the warning signs were everywhere. Valuation ratios were stretched, debt levels were rising, and we were well past the average length of a typical market cycle.

Still, when anyone raised red flags, the pushback was immediate. "Real estate never goes down nationally," people said. "The Fed will not let the market fall." Recent experience had completely overshadowed the broader historical patterns. People were not making irrational arguments. They were just under the spell of what they had most recently lived through.

This failure to weigh base rates does not just affect individual investors. It is everywhere. Economists often predict the next year will look a lot like the last, not because they are lazy, but because our minds tend to extrapolate the recent past. Corporate budgets work the same way. Companies that just had a great year plan for more of the same, often just as the cycle is about to shift.

You saw it happen on a massive scale with Peloton during COVID. With everyone stuck at home, business exploded. Sales skyrocketed, and the stock followed... up over 400 percent in 2020 alone. But management assumed the boom would last. They ramped up manufacturing and inventory like demand would never return to normal. When gyms reopened, they did. The company was left with warehouses full of unsold equipment, and the stock crashed more than 90 percent from its highs.

This is how the base rate fallacy and recency bias feed off each other. We assume that whatever trend we are in is the "new normal," when more often than not, it is just a cycle nearing its end.

The most successful investors and the smartest operators are the ones who stay grounded in base rates. They assume the extraordinary is temporary. They do not chase recent performance. They plan for things to cool down, even during the hottest streaks.

Because in investing, as in life, what is common is more likely than what is exceptional. Ignoring that truth is one of the most expensive mistakes you can make.

The Regression to the Mean Analyzer: A Simple Tool for Clearer Thinking

One of the most valuable tools you can use to fight recency bias is what I call the Regression to the Mean Analyzer. It is not a formula or a model. It is just a way of thinking that helps you stay grounded when emotions or headlines start pulling you in.

Whenever you see an investment that has had an incredible run or an unusually bad stretch, it helps to step back and ask a few key questions. First, how far is this performance from what is historically normal? Are we looking at something truly exceptional, or just a big swing above or below the long-term average?

Next, what has been driving that performance? Is it rooted in something real and lasting, or is it tied to a temporary event or short-term burst of enthusiasm?

And finally, is that driver likely to stick around? Because if it is not, then the odds are high that things will eventually drift back toward the mean (Mauboussin, 2016).

A great example of this in action was Zoom during the pandemic. In 2020, the company's stock exploded, climbing more than 400 percent in a matter of months. At its peak, Zoom was trading at nearly 50 times sales, an eye-popping number even for a high-quality tech company. The driver was obvious: the world suddenly needed video calls more than ever, and Zoom was the go-to platform. But while the company had a great product and a strong brand, the pace of growth was never going to last forever. As vaccinations rolled out and people began returning to offices, demand normalized. Zoom continued to grow, but not at pandemic speed, and the stock price followed suit, falling sharply in the years that followed.

That is exactly what the Regression to the Mean Analyzer is meant to catch. It helps you look past the headlines and ask: is this performance sustainable, or are we likely to see a return to more typical levels? I have used this lens not just with stocks, but across sectors and even in real estate. The key is to distinguish between structural shifts (those rare, lasting changes in how the world works) and cyclical patterns that eventually swing back.

If you do not make that distinction, it is easy to fall into the trap of thinking whatever just happened is what is going to keep happening. In investing, that is often where the biggest mistakes and the biggest missed opportunities come from.

Watch Out When Stock Picking

When you are sizing up a company, one of the biggest warning signs is not buried in a spreadsheet. It is in how management talks about the future. If they are just drawing a straight line from the recent past and assuming more of the same, that is recency bias creeping in. When leaders fall for it, investors often end up holding the bag.

I have learned to listen closely to how executives frame their outlook. Are they honest about where their company stands in the cycle? Do they acknowledge risks like rising competition, slowing demand, or changing market dynamics? Or are they just caught up in recent momentum and acting like it will last forever?

You can usually tell when recency bias is driving the story. Companies start treating short-term windfalls as permanent. They ramp up hiring, open new locations, or launch expensive ventures right after a few good quarters, often with little thought for what might go wrong. You will hear comments like, "We have consistently outperformed, even in tough conditions," as if history is on autopilot. And when things turn, the blame shifts to external forces, never internal missteps.

The smart companies (the ones that manage like good investors) do not operate that way. They expect the unexpected. They know the business world moves in cycles, not straight lines. So, they leave themselves room to adapt. They do not bet the farm after a hot streak, and they do not panic during a slump.

Berkshire Hathaway is a prime example. Buffett has been clear with shareholders that the company's size alone makes it nearly impossible to match the returns of the past. That is not false modesty. It is realism. He knows the bigger you get, the harder it is to move the needle.

Berkshire still makes good investments, but it cannot double in value like it did decades ago... not without taking risks that would compromise what makes it great. That humility and clear-eyed thinking are exactly what protect shareholders over the long run.

Now compare that to companies that get hooked on their own hype. They assume that just because something worked recently, it will keep working forever. So, they chase growth, stretch balance sheets, and expand into untested territory. Then the market shifts, demand cools, and suddenly those big bets do not look so smart.

When you are picking stocks, do not just pore over earnings and ratios. Pay attention to how management thinks. Are they grounded in reality, or just high on recent wins? Are they planning for a range of outcomes, or just hoping the future mirrors the past? Companies that assume every tailwind will last forever usually find themselves overextended. The ones that stay humble, patient, and flexible are the ones worth betting on.

The Market's Memory Problem

Markets have what I like to call a memory problem. They tend to forget their own history. When the collective memory fades, investors start making decisions based entirely on what's happened lately, not on how things have played out over the long run.

You could see this clearly with inflation. For years, decades really, inflation was low and stable across developed economies. So, when signs of rising inflation started to show up in 2021, the consensus response was quick and dismissive. "It's transitory," they said. Economists, central bankers, and most investors leaned on the recent past as their guide. But they overlooked a bigger truth. History tells us that once inflation gains momentum, it tends to stick around and cause problems.

The people who saw through that recency bias, who looked past the last 10 years and paid attention to the last 50, had a chance to position themselves accordingly. When inflation spiked to levels we hadn't seen since the early 1980s, they were rewarded for taking the long view.

Interest rates told a similar story. After the 2008 financial crisis, rates stayed near zero for over a decade. Entire investing strategies were built around the idea that they would stay low forever. The phrase "There Is No Alternative (TINA)" became gospel. Bonds were dismissed, and risk-taking was rewarded. But when rates finally started climbing in 2022, that playbook stopped working. Portfolios built for a zero-rate world struggled badly in a high rate one.

This is the danger of the market's short memory. When everyone starts acting like the recent trend will go on forever, that's often when the trend is most vulnerable to reversing.

And that's where opportunities can arise if you're willing to step back and take the long view. When the crowd is anchored to the recent past, history becomes your edge. Markets may forget, but disciplined investors do not have to.

Adopting a Long-Term Perspective

So how do you protect yourself from recency bias, that powerful tendency to let the recent past shape your entire outlook? The answer isn't to fight your psychology with willpower alone. It's to build habits and systems that help you stay focused on the bigger picture, especially when the short-term noise gets loud.

One of the most effective tools is dollar-cost averaging. It's not flashy, but it works. You invest a fixed amount on a regular schedule, whether the market is booming or crashing. The beauty of this approach is that it strips emotion out of the equation. When markets are falling, it keeps you from freezing in fear. When they're rising, it prevents you from chasing performance.

Recency bias tries to whisper in your ear, "Why invest now? Things are getting worse." Or, "Put more in. Look how fast it's going up." But dollar-cost averaging helps you ignore those voices. You keep investing through the cycle. Over time, you end up buying more shares when prices are low and fewer when prices are high. It's automatic discipline. And just as importantly, it gives you peace of mind. You're not stuck wondering whether now is the right time. You've already committed to the process.

Another powerful system is regular rebalancing. Let's say your portfolio is split between stocks and bonds. After a great year for stocks, they make up a larger portion than you intended. Rebalancing forces you to sell some winners and buy more of the laggards. That's not an easy thing to do, especially when the winners are still getting all the headlines, but it's exactly what keeps your portfolio aligned with your plan.

Another habit that's helped me take a longer view is studying history. I don't just look at what's happened in the last year or two when I'm thinking about investing during high inflation. I go back to the 1970s. I look at how other countries have handled inflationary spikes. I try to understand what's changed and what hasn't.

Market history may not repeat exactly, but it definitely rhymes. Bull markets often end in euphoria. Bear markets end in despair. It's a cycle that plays out over and over, driven largely by human emotion. I keep a chart on my desk showing the typical emotional rollercoaster of markets, starting with optimism, rising through thrill and euphoria, then plunging through fear, panic, and finally back toward hope.

That chart isn't there to predict anything. It's there to remind me that every market feeling I'm experiencing has happened before and will happen again.

Recency bias keeps most investors stuck on that ride. When things are going great, they assume it'll last forever. When things are going poorly, they expect more pain. Either way, they're reacting to what just happened, not preparing for what might come next.

The truth is, you don't need to predict turning points. You just need to recognize your own biases and put guardrails in place to keep you from acting on them. The best investors aren't fortune tellers. They're disciplined. They're self-aware. And most importantly, they've learned how to stay focused on the long game, even when the short-term feels like it's shouting in their face.

The Final Word: Look Further Than Yesterday

Recency bias isn't some academic jargon tucked away in a textbook. It's just human nature, something we all wrestle with, especially when we're making decisions with money on the line. We tend to give too much weight to what just happened, as if the recent past is a crystal ball. It's not. And when we fall into that trap, we often end up making the wrong moves at the worst times.

This bias tricks us into thinking today's market conditions will keep going forever. If stocks are falling, we expect more of the same. If they're soaring, we convince ourselves the good times will roll on. Either way, we lose sight of the big picture.

But here's the good news: once you spot this bias, you can start doing something about it. That's where the real edge comes in. When most investors are glued to the latest headlines, you can choose to zoom out, to think in years, not weeks. That broader view is what sets great investors apart.

Speaking from experience, recognizing recency bias changed the way I invest. I still feel the tug of recent events. Who doesn't? But I've built habits and frameworks that help me step back and stay grounded. Things like sticking to a long-term plan, rebalancing regularly, and studying market history help so I don't get swept up in the drama of the day.

What's tricky is that recency bias doesn't just mess with you once. It sneaks back in, over and over. If you're not careful, it can lead you into a pattern, buying high when things feel good and selling low when they don't. Getting out of that loop means putting real guardrails in place. It's not about having superhuman discipline. It's about having systems that work even when your emotions are running hot.

So, as you keep building your investment approach, remember: yesterday's news is just that. Yesterday's. It matters, but it doesn't tell the whole story. Markets evolve. They surprise us. The future won't look exactly like the past, no matter how tempting it is to believe otherwise.

The investors who succeed over decades are the ones who understand that. They don't chase what just happened. They stay curious, patient, and willing to think beyond the moment. That's the mindset I try to hold on to. And I hope it's one you'll carry forward too.

Chapter Eleven

Practical Tools to Counter Behavioral Biases

L ET ME LEAVE YOU with a simple truth that's easy to forget. The most dangerous place in investing isn't the stock market. It's the space between your ears.

You can read every book, follow the best analysts, and build the perfect spreadsheet. But if your behavior betrays your knowledge, none of it matters. That's the hard part. The market doesn't care how smart you are. It tests how well you can manage your impulses when money is on the line.

Throughout this book, we've looked under the hood of human psychology. We've seen how overconfidence sneaks in wearing a suit of logic, how a compelling story can make us forget the numbers, how losses feel twice as painful as gains feel good, and how crowds can make even calm minds do foolish things.

But naming these biases isn't enough. Knowing your flaws doesn't fix them. The real skill, the edge most investors never develop, is building habits and systems that quietly steer you away from those mistakes. The good news is, you don't need a hundred different tools. A solid decision process, used consistently, can guard you from a whole bunch of psychological pitfalls at once.

What comes next is your toolkit. Not a theory. Not fluff. Just real strategies that some of the world's sharpest and most emotionally aware investors use when the market gets noisy, uncertain, and full of temptation. You don't need to use all of them. Just try to find the ones that work well with your emotions and personality. Trust me. You can avoid costly mistakes with the right processes and systems. At the end of the day, investing isn't about knowing more. It's about behaving better.

The Pre-Mortem: Think About Losing Before You Leap

Here's a trick I wish more investors used, especially before putting serious money on the line. It's called the pre-mortem, and it's dead simple. Before you make an investment, pretend it's already gone south. Then ask yourself, why?

Imagine a year from now, the stock you just bought is down 30%. What happened? What went wrong?

This isn't just a thought exercise. It's a way to outsmart your own brain. The idea comes from research psychologist Gary Klein, who said, "The premortem technique is a sneaky way to get people to do contrarian, devil's advocate thinking without encountering resistance" (Klein, 2007). People don't like being told their plan might fail, but they're more open to testing their own ideas when you flip the frame. By assuming failure and working backwards, you stop being a cheerleader and start being an analyst.

This shift helps in more ways than one. It keeps overconfidence in check. It forces you to seek out what could go wrong instead of just looking for confirming evidence. And it snaps you out of the grip of a good story before you're emotionally sold on it.

And the best part? You don't need a fancy system. Just set aside 15 minutes before you commit to a big investment. Sit down and write out a scenario where you've lost money, 30% or more. Be detailed. Maybe it was a management misstep. Or a market shift. Or a competitor coming out of nowhere. Whatever it is, put it on paper. This isn't paranoia. It's preparation.

Daniel Kahneman, the Nobel Prize-winning psychologist, backs this approach fully. In *Thinking, Fast and Slow*, he wrote, "The main virtue of the premortem is that it legitimizes doubts. It encourages even supporters of the decision to search for possible threats that they had not considered earlier" (Kahneman, 2011). That permission to doubt, before you're financially or emotionally committed, is invaluable.

Just think back to Theranos. Investors were swept up in a compelling vision, sold by a charismatic founder. But a proper pre-mortem might've triggered questions like: What if the technology doesn't work? What if regulators step in? What if someone else solves this problem better? Instead of buying into the dream, they might've asked for evidence and saved themselves billions.

The pre-mortem won't catch every flaw. But it will make you think deeper, ask harder questions, and protect your downside. That is about as close to a superpower as you'll find in investing.

The Process-Outcome Matrix: How to Tell If You Were Smart or Just Lucky

One of the most important tools in any investor's kit is also one of the simplest: figuring out whether a result came from skill or dumb luck. That's where the Process-Outcome Matrix comes in. Developed by investment strategist Michael Mauboussin, this framework breaks your outcomes into four neat boxes. Good process with a good result (deserved win), good process with a bad result (bad luck), bad process with a good result (lucky break), and bad process with a bad result (well, you earned that one).

Mauboussin spells it out clearly in his book *Think Twice*: "In activities where skill and luck both contribute to results, you must focus on process. Over time, a sound process will lead to satisfactory outcomes even if luck works against you periodically" (Mauboussin, 2009). That one quote should be taped to every investor's desk. It's a reminder that the process is what you control, not the outcome.

This idea pushes back hard against outcome bias. That nasty habit we all have of judging a decision based only on how it turned out. It also helps tame attribution bias, which makes us believe every win came from brilliance and every loss was bad luck. But luck, as Mauboussin reminds us, is a lousy teacher. Only process lets you learn and improve.

So how do you actually build a strong process? That's where checklists come in. Charlie Munger, Warren Buffett's right-hand man, has long used mental checklists to stay sharp. In *Poor Charlie's Almanack*, he says, "You need a different checklist and different mental models for different companies... I use a checklist mentally to make sure I'm not making errors of omission" (Munger, 2005). He's not talking about mindless boxes to tick. He's talking about keeping your thinking honest and thorough.

Seth Klarman, one of the most respected value investors around, echoes this in *Margin of Safety*: "A comprehensive investment checklist can help you avoid the omission of crucial factors in the analysis, and can ensure that you've completed all the necessary work before making an investment decision" (Klarman, 1991). A good checklist won't make your process mechanical. It makes it reliable. It keeps you from skipping steps when you're rushed, emotional, or overconfident.

But a checklist is only as useful as the questions you ask. Don't stop at, "Have I considered the risks?" Go further. Ask, "What are the top three threats to this company's future?" Don't just ask, "Do I understand the competition?" Ask, "If this business disappeared tomorrow, who would benefit and what would they do to make that happen?"

This kind of deep questioning protects you from a host of behavioral traps. It counters attribution bias (Chapter 3), helps you resist anchoring bias (Chapter 6), and gives you a way to back out of bad decisions gracefully, without ego. That's commitment escalation from Chapter 7.

Surgeon Atul Gawande, who studied checklists in high-stakes professions, found that even in investing, they made a measurable difference. In *The Checklist Manifesto*, he writes: "Under conditions of complexity, not only are checklists a help, they are required for success... They don't just ensure that the simple stuff is remembered; they make sure the critical but easily overlooked things are not missed" (Gawande, 2009).

And Robert Rubin, former U.S. Treasury Secretary and Goldman Sachs executive, put it best in *In an Uncertain World*: "Any individual decision can be badly thought through, and yet be successful, or exceedingly well thought through, but be unsuccessful... But over time, more thoughtful decision-making will lead to better results" (Rubin, 2003).

When you pair Mauboussin's matrix with a thoughtful checklist, you've got a system that does more than just catch mistakes. It teaches you how to make better decisions, stay humble when things go well, and stay rational when they don't. And that's the kind of edge that compounds over time.

Probabilistic Thinking: Don't Bet the Farm on a Single Future

If there's one mental habit that could save investors from a heap of trouble, it's this: stop pretending you know what's going to happen. Most investing mistakes come from that dangerous illusion of certainty, thinking a stock will go up, or that a specific outcome must play out. The market loves nothing more than proving us wrong.

The antidote is probabilistic thinking. The idea is that the future isn't a single path, but a branching tree of possibilities. Instead of asking, "Will this stock succeed?" start asking, "What are the different ways this could go, and how likely is each one?"

Daniel Kahneman, in *Thinking, Fast and Slow*, hits the nail on the head: "Whenever we can replace thinking about the probability of a single event with thinking about the frequency of such events

in a reference class, we are likely to make more accurate judgments"
(Kahneman, 2011). In other words, step back. Look at similar situations from the past. Think in ranges, not absolutes.

Howard Marks, who's seen more cycles than most of us have had hot dinners, puts it even more plainly in *The Most Important Thing*: "The future should be viewed not as a fixed outcome that's destined to happen and capable of being predicted, but as a range of possibilities and, hopefully on the basis of insight into their respective likelihoods, as a probability distribution" (Marks, 2011). That mindset shift from certainty to probabilities is a superpower in investing.

Of course, thinking this way doesn't come naturally. You have to practice. Start by laying out three realistic scenarios for any investment: a base case (what you think is most likely), a best case, and a worst case. For each one, think about what would have to happen in the company, the industry, or the broader economy to make it real. Then, assign rough probabilities to each. Make sure they add up to 100 percent. Once you've got those, ask yourself: does the weighted average, the expected value, still make this investment worth it?

This approach would have helped during some painful market lessons. Remember Bill Miller's legendary run at Legg Mason? He beat the market 15 years in a row until 2008, when his fund dropped 55 percent, far worse than the S&P 500. The problem wasn't just bad luck. It was betting too heavily on a single story, that financial stocks would keep humming along. No contingency planning. No range of outcomes. Just blind confidence in a narrative that crumbled fast. A little probabilistic thinking might have saved him, or at least softened the blow.

Thinking in probabilities doesn't just protect your downside. It also clears out a lot of behavioral junk. It cools down over-confidence (see Chapter 2), because it forces you to admit you don't know. It breaks narrative bias (see Chapter 5) by replacing tidy stories with messy scenarios. It fights confirmation bias (see Chapter 4) by making you consider ideas you might not like. And it counters recency bias (see Chapter 10) by reminding you that the future doesn't have to look like the recent past.

You won't get the probabilities right every time. That's not the point. The point is to start thinking like a risk manager, not a fortune teller. In the long run, it's not the investor who guesses right that wins. It's the one who prepares for being wrong.

The Decision Journal: Because Your Memory's a Terrible Historian

Let's be honest: we all think we remember things better than we actually do, especially when money is involved. But our memories are slippery. We forget, we revise, and we rewrite stories to make ourselves look a little smarter, a little more rational than we actually were at the time.

That's where a decision journal earns its keep. It's not complicated, just a simple, honest record of what you were thinking when you made an investment decision. No edits, no rewrites. Just the raw, unfiltered version of your reasoning in the moment.

Michael Mauboussin, who's spent a career studying decision-making, describes it well: "The idea is to record your thought process before making a decision, including the variables you consider, your predictions, and your confidence level. Then you can periodically go back and review how well your decisions have turned out" (Mauboussin, 2008). It's not just about judging whether you were right or wrong. It's about judging how you thought.

Guy Spier, in *The Education of a Value Investor*, shares how this works in real life: "I write down what I'm buying or selling, why I'm doing it, and how I feel about it. Later, I check whether the investment decision was good or bad, and more importantly, whether my process was good or bad" (Spier, 2014). That last part — separating the process from the outcome — is key.

You don't need a fancy system. Just a consistent habit. Every time you make a big decision, write down your investment thesis. Why do you believe this company is a good bet? What might make it go south? How confident are you? (Score it from 1 to 10.) What would cause you to sell? And be honest about how you're feeling: excited, nervous, unsure?

Then, this is where the magic happens. Go back and read those entries. Not just when things blow up, but regularly. Set a quarterly reminder. Ask yourself: What actually happened? Where did my thinking go right? Where did I fool myself?

James Montier, in *The Little Book of Behavioral Investing*, puts it plainly: "Decision journals help prevent hindsight bias from distorting our memory of why we made an investment. When we revisit our original logic months later, we're often surprised by the gap between our remembered rationale and what we actually wrote" (Montier, 2010). That gap is where the learning lives.

Journaling helps you face the truth, not just about your winners and losers, but about your thinking patterns. Maybe you always overestimate growth. Maybe you get caught up in flashy narratives. Maybe you're too quick to dismiss competitive threats. The journal brings those blind spots into the light.

It also keeps your ego in check. Remember Bill Ackman's epic short on Herbalife? As losses piled up, he doubled down instead of stepping back. A well-kept decision journal might have helped him see that his thesis was getting weaker, not stronger. Instead of digging in, he could have reevaluated with clearer eyes.

In short, a decision journal won't make your predictions perfect. But it will make your process sharper, your learning deeper, and your decisions more honest. In investing, that's as close to an edge as most of us will ever get.

Portfolio Tranching: Using Mental Accounting to Stay Sane

Mental accounting gets a bad rap in behavioral finance. It's usually framed as a flaw, the way we irrationally treat money differently depending on where it came from or how we've labeled it. But like many quirks of human behavior, if you use it the right way, it can actually help.

That's the idea behind portfolio tranching. Instead of pretending you're a perfectly rational investor with one big pot of money, you split your portfolio into separate "buckets," each with its own purpose, time horizon, and review schedule. It's a psychological trick, yes, but a useful one. It keeps you emotionally steady in choppy markets.

Take a simple structure. Maybe 70 percent of your portfolio is your long-term core. Low-cost index funds, reviewed quarterly, the part you never touch. Another 20 percent goes into a strategic bucket. Individual stocks or sector funds you understand well and check on monthly. The last 10 percent is your tactical sandbox. More speculative plays you review weekly. The exact split doesn't matter as much as the intent: each tranche has its own rules and its own tempo.

Behavioral economist Meir Statman explains why this works: "It helps investors satisfy both their need for protection from devastating losses and their hope for riches" (Statman, 2011). That long-term core gives you stability. The strategic slice lets you explore solid opportunities. And the small tactical chunk scratches the itch to "do something" without risking your whole plan.

This setup quietly solves a few major problems. It counters loss aversion (see Chapter 8) by keeping your riskier bets separate from your financial foundation. It reduces action bias, that nagging urge to tinker with your portfolio just because markets are moving. And it shields your core investments from the emotional whiplash of recency bias (see Chapter 10), which often tempts investors to overreact to the latest headline.

Financial planner Carl Richards puts it well in *The Behavior Gap*: "By dividing your money into different buckets with different time horizons, you create a psychological buffer against making emotional decisions when markets get volatile" (Richards, 2012). That buffer can be the difference between staying calm and making a panic sale at the bottom.

Look back at March 2020, when COVID panic sent markets into a tailspin. Investors who had a tranched setup didn't need to scramble. Their core stayed intact. Maybe they trimmed or added to positions in the tactical bucket. Maybe they took advantage of opportunities in the strategic slice. But they didn't throw the whole plan out the window.

Tranching won't make you immune to market stress, but it creates just enough structure and just enough psychological separation to keep your emotions from hijacking your long-term goals. In investing, that's often the edge that matters most.

The Check-In Calendar: Outsmarting Yourself With a Schedule

One of the sneakiest ways investors sabotage themselves is by constantly checking their portfolios. Every glance becomes a chance to react, and the more often you look, the more likely you are to overreact.

Research backs this up. In a landmark study published in the *Quarterly Journal of Economics*, Shlomo Benartzi and Richard Thaler found that "frequent evaluation of investment performance leads to excessive sensitivity to short-term losses, and hence to lower risk-taking" (Benartzi & Thaler, 1995). In simple terms, if you check your portfolio every day, the ups and downs feel way bigger, and you start seeing safe investments as riskier than they actually are.

So how do you protect yourself from yourself? Create a check-in calendar. Set fixed dates, maybe once a quarter for long-term investments, and once a month for shorter-term or higher-risk stuff. In between those dates, don't look. Seriously. Treat those calendar check-ins like doctor appointments. Firm, not flexible.

At first, this might feel like swimming against the current. But over time, it becomes a habit. Some investors even use tools to enforce the rule, such as password managers that only unlock brokerage accounts on scheduled days, or having a spouse or friend hold the login info.

William Bernstein, the neurologist-turned-financial advisor, swears by this method. In *The Four Pillars of Investing*, he writes: "Schedule regular portfolio reviews on your calendar, and avoid looking at your investments between those dates. This simple discipline can dramatically improve your long-term returns" (Bernstein, 2010). And that's coming from someone who's studied both the brain and the markets.

This strategy calms a lot of the usual emotional storms. It reduces loss aversion (see Chapter 7), because you're not watching your portfolio bounce around every day. It fights recency bias (see Chapter 9) by giving you space from the latest headlines. And it helps curb action bias, that twitchy need to do something, by giving you a plan and a reason to wait.

Think back to the GameStop frenzy (see Chapter 8). People glued to their screens were way more likely to get caught in the chaos, buying at the peak and panicking on the way down. But if you had a check-in scheduled a few weeks later, you probably watched it all unfold from the sidelines, then looked at the numbers with a clearer head when your review came up.

The check-in calendar isn't about being passive. It's about being intentional. It gives your investments the breathing room they need to work and gives you the mental space to stay calm when the market isn't.

Active Disconfirmation: Don't Just Argue Your Case. Try to Break It

If you want a real edge in investing, here's something most people won't do: look for reasons you're wrong. Not a hope-you-don't-find-any kind of looking, but actively trying to poke holes in your own ideas and listening closely to those who disagree with you.

This habit, called active disconfirmation, is one of the sharpest tools against confirmation bias. That sneaky tendency to only notice the facts that support your view while ignoring everything else.

Ray Dalio, founder of Bridgewater Associates, doesn't just talk about this idea. He built his entire firm around it. In *Principles*, he writes: "The biggest mistake you can make is to let your emotions override your good decision-making. Seek out the smartest people who disagree with you so you can try to understand their reasoning" (Dalio, 2017). That's not just theory. It's how the world's largest hedge fund stays grounded.

This kind of thinking goes beyond just being open-minded. It means putting real effort into finding the other side of the trade. If you're bullish on a stock, read the best bear case you can find. Follow people who challenge your investing style. Write down what would have to happen to prove your thesis wrong and take those risks seriously. Even better, ask a smart friend to play devil's advocate. It's uncomfortable, but incredibly valuable.

Harvard psychologist Max Bazerman puts it plainly in *The Power of Noticing*: "Most people search for confirming rather than disconfirming evidence. By reversing this natural tendency, you dramatically improve decision quality" (Bazerman, 2014). That little reversal from "how am I right?" to "how might I be wrong?" can be a game-changer.

This habit doesn't just fight confirmation bias (see Chapter 4). It also humbles overconfidence (see Chapter 2) by exposing blind spots. It keeps narrative bias (see Chapter 5) in check by making you question compelling stories. And it helps with commitment escalation (see Chapter 7), giving you a way to exit a bad idea gracefully when the facts no longer support it.

Just think back to Bill Ackman's crusade against Herbalife. As he doubled down, year after year, his conviction turned into a bubble of isolation. Now compare that with how Buffett and Munger have operated for decades. Their success isn't just about being smart. It's about challenging each other's ideas constantly. That partnership works because they're not afraid to say, "I think you might be wrong. Let's talk about it."

Active disconfirmation won't always feel good, but it will make you sharper, more open-minded, and over time, a far better investor.

The Counterfactual Exercise: What Else Could Have Happened?

One of the brain's favorite tricks after an investment plays out, especially if it went well, is to rewrite history. We tell ourselves the outcome was obvious all along. "Of course, that stock doubled. I saw it coming." But more often than not, that's hindsight bias talking, not clear thinking.

The best way to fight it is to use counterfactual thinking. After any investment, win or lose, take a moment to imagine how things could have turned out differently. What if the market hadn't recovered? What if a key competitor had launched first? What if a regulatory curveball had hit? It sounds simple, but it forces your brain out of storytelling mode and into reality-check mode.

Behavioral scientist Philip Tetlock, who has studied forecasting more than just about anyone, emphasizes this point in *Superforecasting*. He writes, "Counterfactual thinking helps combat outcome bias by separating process quality from pure randomness" (Tetlock & Gardner, 2015). In other words, just because something worked doesn't mean it was a good decision, and just because something failed doesn't mean it was a bad one.

So, here's the move: after a winning investment, list three believable scenarios that could have sunk it. Maybe the Fed tightened too soon. Maybe a big competitor launched a better product. Maybe a global event could have slowed demand. And after a loss, ask what parts of your thesis were actually right. Was the business solid but the timing off? Was the strategy sound but the market fickle?

Richard Thaler backs this up in *Nudge*, warning that "judging decisions by their outcomes leads to systematic errors in learning" (Thaler & Sunstein, 2008). You learn more by analyzing your process and imagining how luck might have swung the other way than by patting yourself on the back or beating yourself up.

This method hits multiple behavioral biases at once. It pushes back on hindsight bias (see Chapter 2), keeps attribution bias in check by teasing apart luck and skill, and tamps down overconfidence (see Chapter 1) by reminding you that uncertainty is always part of the game.

Think about the dot-com bubble. A lot of investors back then were right about the internet changing everything, but they still got crushed. Why? Because they didn't game out alternative timelines. What if adoption took longer? What if capital dried up? What if profits stayed elusive? A little counterfactual thinking could have helped them balance conviction with caution and maybe saved their portfolios in the process.

The market doesn't care how confident you are or how clear the story feels in hindsight. What matters is whether you're thinking clearly before and after the fact. Counterfactuals help you do just that.

The Clean Slate Method: Would You Buy It Again Today?

Here's a simple question that can tell you a lot about your portfolio: If I didn't already own this investment, would I buy it today at this price?

That one question cuts right through a mess of mental fog, and that's what the Clean Slate Method is all about. It's a technique for seeing your portfolio clearly, without all the baggage that comes from past decisions, price anchors, or emotional attachment.

Richard Thaler and Cass Sunstein talk about this in *Nudge* when they describe "resetting reference points," deliberately stepping back to view decisions as if you were starting fresh (Thaler & Sunstein, 2008). It's a great way to break the mental inertia that keeps us locked into old choices.

Here's how to do it: once a quarter, go through each holding and ask yourself that tough question. Would I buy it again today? If the answer is no, ask the follow-up: Then why am I still holding it? If the only reasons you can come up with are "I've already lost too much" or "I've held it this long," you might be hanging on for the wrong reasons.

Jason Zweig, who has spent a career studying investor behavior, puts it well in *Your Money and Your Brain*: "This simple mental exercise forces you to evaluate investments on their current merits rather than your historical relationship with them" (Zweig, 2007). That's crucial, because the market doesn't care how long you've owned a stock and neither should you.

The Clean Slate Method hits several key biases at once. It helps shake off anchoring bias (see Chapter 5) because you stop fixating on your original purchase price. It tackles loss aversion (see Chapter 7) by shifting your focus from what's already gone to what the future looks like. And it helps stop commitment escalation (see Chapter 6), that dangerous urge to double down just to prove you were right.

Think about the case of General Electric we discussed in Chapter 6. A lot of investors stuck with GE far too long, not because they still believed in its future, but because they were emotionally anchored to its past or to the price they originally paid. A Clean Slate review might have sparked a tougher question: Would I buy GE today if I didn't already own it? For many, the honest answer would have been "no," and that answer could have saved years of frustration.

This isn't about second-guessing everything. It's about building the habit of fresh thinking. Because the best investors aren't the ones who never make mistakes; they're the ones who know when to walk away from them.

Regular Rebalancing: A Built-In Way to Buy Low and Sell High

If there's a behavioral tool that deserves more respect, it's regular rebalancing. It's not flashy. It won't win you any bragging rights at a dinner party. But quietly, in the background, it can be one of the smartest moves you make as an investor.

The idea is simple: you decide on a mix of investments that fits your goals. Maybe 60 percent stocks, 40 percent bonds, and then, at regular intervals or when those weights drift too far, you reset them. That means selling a bit of what's done well and buying more of what's lagged. Emotionally, it's hard to do, which is exactly why it works.

John Bogle, the founder of Vanguard and one of the great voices of common sense in investing, summed it up nicely in *The Little Book of Common Sense Investing*: "Rebalancing is a simple discipline that can have profound effects on your long-term returns, primarily by controlling risk but also by enforcing a sell-high, buy-low approach without requiring market timing" (Bogle, 2007). In other words, it's a quiet way to do something most investors struggle with: act like a contrarian when it matters most.

The beauty of rebalancing is that it takes the emotion out of the decision. You don't have to sit there in the middle of a market panic trying to figure out what to do. The plan's already set. You're just following the rules you made back when your head was clear.

You can rebalance on a schedule, say, quarterly or yearly, or when things drift a certain percentage from your targets. Either way, the mechanics are simple: trim the winners, top up the losers, and bring your portfolio back in line.

And here's the kicker: research from Morningstar shows that investors who rebalance consistently outperform those who don't by about 0.5 percent per year (Morningstar, 2018). That may not sound like much, but over decades, it adds up. And it's not because they picked better stocks. It's because they stayed disciplined when others didn't.

Rebalancing tackles several behavioral biases at once. It keeps recency bias (see Chapter 9) in check by preventing you from piling into whatever just had a good run. It helps manage loss aversion (see Chapter 7) by nudging you to buy what's down, not what feels safe. And it quietly resists the herd mentality (see Chapter 8), pulling you away from the crowd when it matters most.

Look at the dot-com bubble. From 1998 to 1999, tech stocks were flying, and anyone with a diversified portfolio saw their allocations shift toward tech whether they meant to or not. Rebalancing during that time meant selling some of those high-fliers. Painful in the moment but wise in hindsight. Then when the market tanked in the early 2000s, rebalancers were the ones buying back in at much lower prices. They weren't trying to time the market. They were just sticking to a plan.

Regular rebalancing won't make you feel like a genius in the short term, but it will help you behave like one over time. And in investing, behavior beats brilliance almost every time.

The Contrarian Calendar: Planning to Be Brave When It's Hard

Everyone knows the Buffett line: "Be fearful when others are greedy, and greedy when others are fearful." But let's be honest. That's a lot easier to say than to actually do.

When markets are crashing and headlines are screaming doom, most of us freeze or flee. When stocks are soaring, we get swept up in the euphoria. The problem isn't that we don't know what to do. It's that our emotions overpower our logic when the stakes are high.

That's where the Contrarian Calendar comes in. It's a tool to help you make bold decisions when others can't, not by being smarter in the moment, but by preparing in advance.

Howard Marks, one of the most respected value investors out there, champions this approach. In *The Most Important Thing*, he writes: "You can't predict. You can prepare" (Marks, 2011). That's the essence of this strategy — preparing your moves ahead of time so you're not left scrambling in a crisis.

Here's how it works: you set predefined triggers for different market conditions, downturns, rallies, or whatever matters to your plan. For example, if the market drops 10 percent from its peak, maybe you commit to investing 25 percent of your available cash. If it drops 20 percent, invest another 25 percent. Keep going at 30 percent and 40 percent. It's not about calling the bottom. It's about committing to act as the market moves.

You can flip this for exuberant markets too. Maybe you reduce exposure or raise cash as valuations climb beyond your comfort zone. The key is to plan these decisions when your head is clear, not when your heart is racing.

And it works. A study published in the *Journal of Portfolio Management* found that rule-based contrarian strategies consistently outperformed both market indices and investors' own results from before they used the strategy. The reason wasn't better timing. It was avoiding bad timing driven by emotion (Campbell R. Harvey, 2020).

This strategy hits multiple behavioral blind spots. It counters herd mentality (see Chapter 9) by giving you a structured plan to go against the crowd. It beats recency bias (see Chapter 10) by reminding you that just because something's falling doesn't mean it's broken. And it helps you deal with loss aversion (see Chapter 8) by automating the tough decisions before fear can take over.

Look back at March 2020. Markets dropped over 30 percent in a matter of weeks. Fear was everywhere. Most people panicked or stayed frozen. But investors who had set a contrarian calendar were stepping in, not with bravado, but with a plan. They didn't need courage in the moment. They just needed to stick to what they'd already decided.

The Contrarian Calendar doesn't guarantee perfect timing. But it does give you a way to act with clarity when others can't. And that edge can be worth more than any market forecast.

The Dry Powder Discipline

One of the smartest habits an investor can develop is keeping some cash on hand, not out of fear, but out of patience. This is the idea behind dry powder discipline. It's about having money set aside specifically for moments when the market goes haywire and everyone else is paralyzed by fear.

Warren Buffett is a master of this. People often forget that Berkshire Hathaway isn't just an insurance conglomerate. It's also a giant war chest. Even after accounting for the cash needed to cover Berkshire's insurance operations, Buffett has kept tens of billions of dollars sitting idle. Not because he can't find any investments, but because he's waiting for the right ones. As of recent years, Berkshire has held more than $300 billion in cash, well beyond the company's operational needs.

Why? Because Buffett knows something that many investors overlook: the best opportunities show up when no one else can take advantage of them. In a panic, prices drop faster than logic. If you've got dry powder, you're not scrambling to sell something else or wondering whether to throw in fresh capital. You're ready to strike.

And here's where the real value shows up: psychology. If you don't have cash set aside, buying during a downturn feels like doubling down on risk. You're either selling something else to make room or you're putting in new money when everything feels like it's collapsing. But when you've earmarked cash for exactly this kind of moment, you're not reacting. You're executing. It's the difference between impulse and strategy.

Shelby Davis, the little-known investor who turned $50,000 into $900 million, used to call market crashes "sales" and kept cash specifically to shop during them. Buffett's doing the same thing on a much bigger scale. By holding cash, he's not playing defense. He's sitting in the batter's box, waiting for a fat pitch. And when it comes, he swings hard.

Dry powder isn't dead money. It's optionality. It's the ability to act when others can't. And that ability, over a long investing life, is worth far more than a few extra percentage points during bull markets.

The Dhandho Framework: Betting Big When the Downside's Small

If you're looking for a way to stack the odds in your favor, the Dhandho Framework is one of the most practical investing mindsets out there. Mohnish Pabrai, a student of Buffett and author of *The Dhandho Investor*, sums it up with a line that's stuck with me ever since I first read it: "Heads, I win; tails, I don't lose much" (Pabrai, 2007).

This isn't about trying to outsmart your psychological biases. It's about structuring your investments so that those biases don't have as much room to do damage. If you're mostly protected on the downside, your emotions don't get triggered as easily. You're not sweating every tick of the market when you know your worst-case scenario isn't catastrophic.

At its core, the Dhandho Framework is built around four ideas. First, you focus on the downside before you get excited about the upside. Ask: what could go wrong? How much could I realistically lose? If the worst-case isn't survivable, walk away. Second, look for mispriced bets, situations where the upside is big but the market's fear or misunderstanding has made the price cheap. Third, keep it simple. If you don't understand the business, don't invest. Complexity hides risk. And fourth, be patient. Wait for the fat pitches, the rare opportunities where the odds are heavily in your favor.

Warren Buffett's version of this idea is famously blunt: "Rule No. 1: Never lose money. Rule No. 2: Never forget Rule No. 1" (Buffett, 2006). He doesn't mean you'll never take a hit. He means your first priority is always to avoid permanent capital loss, the kind you don't bounce back from. If you build from that mindset, the wins tend to take care of themselves.

This approach does a great job of protecting you from the psychological traps we've been talking about. It dampens overconfidence (see Chapter 2), because you start every analysis with, "What could go wrong?" It keeps narrative bias (see Chapter 5) in check by asking you to focus on facts and downside risk instead of a good story. And it helps tame loss aversion (see Chapter 8), because if you've structured the downside right, you're less likely to panic when things get bumpy.

A classic example is Buffett's investment in American Express during the Salad Oil Scandal of 1963. The stock got crushed. Investors feared massive liabilities. But Buffett dug in and looked at the worst-case scenario, not just the headlines. He decided that while the company would take a hit, its core brand and business were still solid. He saw limited downside and huge upside if the panic passed, and it did. That one investment paid off in spades.

The Dhandho mindset isn't flashy. It's not about swinging for the fences every time. It's about making sure that when you swing, the downside is manageable and the upside is meaningful. And in a game where avoiding big mistakes matters more than chasing big wins, that's a pretty good way to play.

Building Your Personal System: Start Small, Stay Honest

Let's be clear right from the start. You don't need to adopt every tool and tactic we've talked about. In fact, trying to do everything at once is a great way to do nothing at all. The goal here isn't perfection. It's steady progress.

Start with some honest reflection. Go back through your investing track record. Not just the losing trades, but the ones where your thinking felt off. Maybe you bailed too early when a stock dipped. Maybe you fell for a great story and ignored the red flags. Maybe you bought into the hype just because everyone else seemed to be doing it.

Look for patterns. Ask yourself what kinds of decisions trip you up. Where does emotion tend to creep in? Once you've spotted the trouble areas, pick two or three tools that speak directly to them. If compelling stories tend to cloud your judgment (hello, narrative bias from Chapter 4), try the pre-mortem or active disconfirmation. If fear of losses keeps you on the sidelines or causes panic selling (classic loss aversion from Chapter 7), portfolio tranching or a check-in calendar can help you stay grounded.

Ray Dalio, who's built his entire investment philosophy around psychological awareness, puts it this way in *Principles*: "I believe that you can probably get what you want out of life if you can suspend your ego and take a no-excuses approach to achieving your goals with open-mindedness, determination, and courage" (Dalio, 2017). That mindset is as important as any financial model.

Becoming a more psychologically intelligent investor is about doing the small things, consistently. Each time you override a bias, each time you stick to your plan instead of reacting emotionally, those little wins add up. They compound, just like returns.

Don't forget: everyone, even the greats, gets caught in these traps. The difference is in how quickly they notice, how well they adapt, and how faithfully they use systems to keep their emotions in check.

Howard Marks nails it in *The Most Important Thing*: "The biggest challenge for investors is... not letting the mood swings of the market infect you with euphoria or depression" (Marks, 2011). The techniques we've covered won't make those market mood swings disappear. But they will help you handle them better, with more awareness, more calm, and more consistency.

And that, more than any hot stock or market prediction, is what separates great investors from average ones. Not a genius. Not crystal balls. Just clearer thinking and steadier behavior, repeated over time.

Beyond Returns: The Edge That Lasts

We began this journey with a simple truth: the biggest challenges in investing aren't technical. They're psychological. Overconfidence, seductive stories, fear-driven decisions. These aren't market problems. They're human ones. And yet, as we've seen, there are tools to manage them. Pre-mortems. Decision journals. Rebalancing routines. Portfolio check-ins. Each one designed not to predict the future, but to help you navigate it with a clearer mind.

But now, as we close, it's time to zoom out. Because the value of psychological intelligence in investing goes far beyond your portfolio.

The first change you'll feel is subtle but profound: peace. Markets will still swing. Fear will still show up. But it won't run the show anymore. You'll have systems in place that create space between emotion and action, and that space is everything. Suddenly, volatility becomes noise, not danger. You stop reacting and start responding. That shift alone can transform your financial life.

And it doesn't stop there. These same patterns (loss aversion, sunk cost bias, narrative fallacy) show up everywhere. In business. In relationships. In career moves and big purchases. Learning to think clearly under pressure isn't just an investing skill. It's a life skill. And once you build it, it follows you.

You'll notice something else, too. The more you internalize these ideas, the more you'll want to share them. Whether you're mentoring your kids, guiding friends, or coaching younger investors, you now have something rare to offer: a roadmap. Not just for growing wealth, but for avoiding the painful detours that often come first. That kind of wisdom is a gift, one that only comes from experience and reflection.

Most importantly, this journey turns investing into something deeper than just a way to build capital. It becomes a path of personal development. Because to invest well, you have to know yourself. You have to face your emotions, question your stories, and build habits that keep you grounded. You learn to stay steady when things get noisy. To make decisions with clarity, even when the stakes feel high. That kind of growth lasts far longer than any bull market.

In a world obsessed with speed, complexity, and forecasts, it's easy to miss the real secret: the best investors aren't always the smartest. They're the most self-aware. They don't need to be right all the time. They just need to avoid the worst mistakes, stay calm under pressure, and stick to a process they trust.

Charlie Munger said it best: "It is remarkable how much long-term advantage people like us have gotten by trying to be consistently not stupid, instead of trying to be very intelligent." That's the bar. Not brilliance. Not perfect timing. Just clear thinking, done consistently, over time.

In that sense, your greatest edge isn't some trick or tactic. It's your ability to see the gap between what you know and what you do, and to build the discipline to close it.

That edge doesn't expire. It doesn't get disrupted. It can't be outsourced or automated away. It lives in the space between reason and reaction, between emotion and execution. It's the rarest kind of advantage: one that's available to anyone but claimed by few.

So, as you go forward, remember: the market doesn't care how clever you are. It rewards clarity. It rewards patience. And above all, it rewards those who can keep their heads when everyone else is losing theirs.

That's the edge. Durable. Repeatable. Yours to earn. The returns will come. But what you'll gain along the way (calm, confidence, self-awareness) is worth even more.

That's not just a better way to invest. It's a better way to live.

Chapter Twelve

BONUS: The Behavioral Investor Toolkit

B Y NOW, YOU'VE SEEN the psychological tools that can separate great investors from the rest of the crowd. But there's
a world of difference between knowing about these biases and
actually having a way to counter them when your money is on
the line.

It's one thing to nod along when someone talks about doing
a pre-mortem. It sounds smart on paper. But what does it look
like when you're feeling excited and tempted to load up on Tesla
shares? The same goes for decision journals. The idea makes sense,
but when Netflix is falling off a cliff and your gut tells you to hit
the sell button, what do you actually write down? This is where
theory meets reality, and where many investors get tripped up.

I know how easy it is to let emotions run the show. That's why I built these behavioral tools into a step-by-step system you can actually use. This isn't just theory or vague advice. It's the checklists, the templates, and the stories from real investors who faced tough choices. I wanted to create a toolkit that shows exactly how to use these tools when you need them most.

If you want to go a step further, I've put everything into "The Behavioral Investor's Toolkit." It's a practical, no-nonsense guide you can download for free. Inside, you'll find the full playbook from what to ask yourself before you buy, to how to stay steady when your stocks are swinging up and down, to knowing when it's time to walk away. Each part comes with real-world stock examples and the same simple checklist I use myself.

At the end of the day, it's not enough just to know what you should do. The key is being able to do it when your instincts are screaming at you to act. That's what this toolkit is all about: giving you a way to keep your head clear and your process steady when things get noisy.

You can grab your copy by following the link below. There's no cost. You'll get the whole toolkit to use whenever you need a little help steering through the emotional storms of investing. Thank you.

https://buffettinvesting.com/books/psychology-of-stock-investing/

Bibliography

(FINRA), F. I. R. A., 2021. 2020 FINRA Industry Snapshot, s.l.: FINRA.

Ashworth, E. M. a. M., 2021. Archegos Was Too Big for Its Banks. Bloomberg Opinion.

Bezos, J., 1997. 1997 Letter to Shareholders. s.l.:Amazon.com Inc..

Blumer, H. R. A. a. C., 1985. The Psychology of Sunk Cost. Organizational Behavior and Human Decision Processes, 35(1), 124-140.

Boyd, R., 2015. The King's Gambit Accepted: The Valeant/Philidor Relationship. Southern Investigative Reporting Foundation.

Buffett, W., 1986. Letter to Shareholders of Berkshire Hathaway Inc., s.l.: Berkshire Hathaway Inc..

Buffett, W., 1990. Letter to Shareholders of Berkshire Hathaway Inc., s.l.: Berkshire Hathaway Inc..

Buffett, W., 1996. Letter to Shareholders of Berkshire Hathaway Inc.. s.l.:Berkshire Hathaway Inc..

Buffett, W., 2006. 2006 Letter to Shareholders, s.l.: Berkshire Hathaway Inc..

Burton, K., 2015. Druckenmiller Calls Dot-Com Era 'Abortion,' Backs Icahn on Apple. Bloomberg.

Business, S. G. S. o., 2013. Ron Johnson: Lessons Learned from Apple and JCPenney [Interview] 2013.

Campbell R. Harvey, S. R. a. O. V. H., 2020. Strategic Risk Management: Designing Portfolios and Managing Risk. Wiley.

Carreyrou, J., 2015. Hot Startup Theranos Has Struggled With Its Blood-Test Technology. The Wall Street Journal.

Cheng, E., 2017. Long Island Iced Tea shares go gangbusters after changing its name to Long Blockchain. CNBC.

Clifford, S., 2012. The Trials of a Transition at J.C. Penney. The New York Times.

Dalio, R., 2017. Principles: Life and Work. s.l.:Simon & Schuster.

Duke, A., 2018. Thinking in Bets: Making Smarter Decisions When You Don't Have All the Facts. s.l.:Portfolio.

Dunbar, N., 2000. The Story of Long-Term Capital Management and the Legends. s.l.:Wiley.

Egan, M., 2018. GE slashes 119-year-old dividend to a penny. CNN Business.

Elkind, B. M. a. P., 2003. The Smartest Guys in the Room: The Amazing Rise and Scandalous Fall of Enron. s.l.:Portfolio.

Featherstone, L., 2006. Wal-Mart's German Retreat. The Nation.

Fitzgerald, F. S., 1936. The Crack-Up. Esquire Magazine.

Gara, A., 2015. Bill Ackman Thinks Valeant Is 'Incredibly Disciplined,' And A Lot Like Early Berkshire Hathaway. Forbes.

Gawande, A., 2009. The Checklist Manifesto: How to Get Things Right. s.l.:Metropolitan Books.

Gawande, A., 2009. The Checklist Manifesto: How to Get Things Right. s.l.:Metropolitan Books.

Goldstein, M., 2008. The Stock Picker's Defeat. Reuters.

Goldstein, M., 2012. Ackman Outlines Bet Against Herbalife. The New York Times.

Graham, B., 1949. The Intelligent Investor. s.l.:Harper Business.

Gregory Zuckerman, J. O. a. J. C., 2021. The Meltdown That Wasn't: How Archegos Capital's Collapse Didn't Tank the Market. The Wall Street Journal.

Herper, M., 2016. From $4.5 Billion To Nothing: Forbes Revises Estimated Net Worth Of Theranos Founder Elizabeth Holmes. Forbes.

Inc., B. H., 2016. Form 13F, s.l.: Securities and Exchange Commission.

Jopson, B., 2011. JCPenney shares jump on CEO appointment. Financial Times.

Juliet Chung, M. P. a. M. F., 2021. Ex-Tiger Asia Founder Bill Hwang Behind Major Morgan Stanley Block Trades. The Wall Street Journal.

Justice, U. D. o., 2021. Trevor Milton, Founder of Nikola Corporation, Charged with Securities and Wire Fraud. s.l.:U.S. Attorney's Office, Southern District of New York.

Kafka, P., 2022. Netflix's growth has finally hit a wall. Vox.

Kahneman, D., 2011. Thinking, Fast and Slow. s.l.:Farrar, Straus and Giroux.

Kate Kelly, M. G. M. P. a. T. S. B., 2021. Robinhood, Under the Gun, Raises $2.4 Billion. The New York Times.

Katherine Burton, S. N. a. G. T., 2021. Bill Hwang Was a $20 Billion Whale, Then Lost It All in Two Days. Bloomberg.

Kinnel, R., 2020. Mind the Gap: Global Investor Returns Show the Costs of Bad Timing Around the World, s.l.: Morningstar.

Klarman, S. A., 1991. Margin of Safety: Risk-Averse Value Investing Strategies for the Thoughtful Investor. s.l.:HarperCollins.

Klein, G., 2007. Performing a Project Premortem. New York: Harvard Business Review.

Klein, G., 2013. Seeing What Others Don't: The Remarkable Ways We Gain Insights. New York: PublicAffairs.

Kochkodin, B., 2021. GameStop Closes With 400% Gain This Week in Win for Reddit Army. Bloomberg.

Kolodny, L., 2020. Nikola admits demo in promotional video was rolling downhill. CNBC.

Loeb, W., 2013. Ron Johnson Out At JCPenney: The Board Calls It Quits. Forbes.

Lowenstein, R., 2000. When Genius Failed: The Rise and Fall of Long-Term Capital Management. s.l.:Random House.

Lynch, P., 1989. One Up on Wall Street. s.l.:Simon & Schuster.

Magazine, F., 1974. Look at All Those Beautiful, Scantily Clad Girls Out There!. Forbes.

Mann, T. G. a. T., 2020. Lights Out: Pride, Delusion, and the Fall of General Electric. Houghton Mifflin Harcourt.

Mann, T. G. a. T., 2020. Lights Out: Pride, Delusion, and the Fall of General Electric. s.l.:Houghton Mifflin Harcourt.

Marks, H., 2011. The Most Important Thing: Uncommon Sense for the Thoughtful Investor. s.l.:Columbia University Press.

Mauboussin, M. J., 2009. Think Twice: Harnessing the Power of Counterintuition. s.l.:Harvard Business Press.

Mauboussin, M. J., 2016. Mean Reversion and Reflexivity, s.l.: Credit Suisse.

Maureen Farrell, M. P. a. J. C., 2021. What Is Archegos and How Did It Rattle the Stock Market?. The Wall Street Journal.

McLean, B., 2016. The Valeant Meltdown and Wall Street's Major Drug Problem. Vanity Fair.

McNamara, R. S., 1995. In Retrospect: The Tragedy and Lessons of Vietnam. s.l.:Times Books.

Mintz, J. N. w. S. L., 1999. John Neff on Investing. s.l.:Wiley.

Montier, J., 2010. The Little Book of Behavioral Investing: How Not to Be Your Own Worst Enemy. s.l.:Wiley.

Munger, C. T., 2005. Poor Charlie's Almanack: The Wit and Wisdom of Charles T. Munger. s.l.:Walsworth Publishing Company.

Mussweiler, A. D. G. a. T., 2001. First Offers as Anchors: The Role of Perspective-Taking and Negotiator Focus. Journal of Personality and Social Psychology, 81(4), 657-669.

Odean, B. M. B. a. T., 2000. Trading Is Hazardous to Your Wealth: The Common Stock Investment Performance of Individual Investors. Journal of Finance, 55(2), 773-806.

Pabrai, M., 2007. The Dhandho Investor: The Low-Risk Value Method to High Returns. s.l.:Wiley.

Parloff, R., 2015. How Theranos Misled Me. Fortune Magazine.

Research, H., 2020. Nikola: How to Parlay An Ocean of Lies Into a Partnership With the Largest Auto OEM in America, s.l.: Hindenburg Research.

Roumeliotis, G., 2013. Buffett says he's harvested $3.1 billion from his Goldman bet. Reuters.

Rubin, R. E., 2003. In an Uncertain World: Tough Choices from Wall Street to Washington. s.l.:Random House.

Sheehan, N., 1988. A Bright Shining Lie: John Paul Vann and America in Vietnam. s.l.:Random House.

Sorkin, A. R., 2008. Buffett's Goldman Deal Is Viewed as a Sign of Confidence. The New York Times.

Soros, G., 2003. The Alchemy of Finance. s.l.:Wiley.

Spier, G., 2014. The Education of a Value Investor. s.l.:Palgrave Macmillan.

Steitz, C., 2020. Tesla's market value set to overtake the combined worth of GM and Ford. Reuters.

Stertz, B. V. a. B. A., 2000. Taken for a Ride: How Daimler-Benz Drove Off With Chrysler. s.l.:William Morrow.

Stevenson, M. G. a. A., 2015. Ackman Defends Valeant Again and Details Steps for Its Recovery. The New York Times.

Stoner, J. A. F., 1961. A comparison of individual and group decisions involving risk. Massachusetts Institute of Technology, School of Industrial Management.

Sushil Bikhchandani, D. H. a. I. W., 1992. A Theory of Fads, Fashion, Custom, and Cultural Change as Informational Cascade. Journal of Political Economy, 100(5), 992-1026.

Swisher, K., 2003. There Must Be a Pony in Here Somewhere: The AOL Time Warner Debacle and the Quest for a Digital Future. s.l.:Crown Business.

TEDMED, 2014. Elizabeth Holmes: Transforming healthcare through revolutionary blood analytics. s.l., TEDMED 2014 Conference.

Tetlock, P. E. &. G. D., 2015. Superforecasting: The Art and Science of Prediction. s.l.:Crown.

Tetlock, P. E., 2005. Expert Political Judgment: How Good Is It? How Can We Know?. s.l.:Princeton University Press.

Thaler, S. B. a. R. H., 1995. Myopic Loss Aversion and the Equity Premium Puzzle. The Quarterly Journal of Economics, 110(1), 73-92.

Vardi, N., 2017. Bill Ackman Sells Valeant Stake After $3 Billion Loss. Forbes.

Vitaly Meursault, P. L. B. R. a. M. W., 2022. The Role of Mobile Devices in the Retail Investor Revolution. SSRN Electronic Journal.

Wahba, P., 2019. Best Buy CEO Hubert Joly Has Done What Amazon Couldn't. Fortune.

Wang, C., 2018. Bill Ackman is finally cashing out of his disastrous $1 billion bet against Herbalife. CNBC.

Wapner, S., 2018. When the Wolves Bite: Two Billionaires, One Company, and an Epic Wall Street Battle. s.l.:PublicAffairs.

Zavalloni, S. M. a. M., 1969. The group as a polarizer of attitudes. Journal of Personality and Social Psychology, 12(2), 125-135.

This page is intentionally left blank.

This page is intentionally left blank.

This page is intentionally left blank.

www.ingramcontent.com/pod-product-compliance
Lightning Source LLC
Chambersburg PA
CBHW071558210326
41597CB00019B/3302